the way they learn

FOCUS ON THE FAMILY®

the way they learn

Cynthia Ulrich Tobias

TYNDALE

Tyndale House Publishers, Wheaton, Illinois

THE WAY THEY LEARN

Tobias, Cynthia Ulrich, 1953–
    The way they learn / Cynthia Ulrich Tobias.
        p. cm.
    Includes bibliographical references.
        ISBN 1-56179-414-7
        1. Learning.   2. cognitive styles in children.   I. Title.
LB1060.T63   1993
370.15'23—dc20   94-14104
                                                              CIP

The terms: *Concrete Sequential, Abstract Sequential, Abstract Random,* and *Concrete Random,* are used with the permission of Anthony F. Gregorc, Ph.D.

A Focus on the Family Book Published by
Tyndale House Publishers, Wheaton, Illinois 60189

Editor: Gwen Weising
Cover design: Jeff Stoddard

Printed in the United States of America
    00 01 02 03 / 26 25 24 23 22 21 20 19 18

Dedication

To my parents, Robert and Minnie Ulrich,
who have always believed the best of me;
my husband, John, who is my staunchest supporter;
and my twin sons, Michael and Robert,
who daily remind me that
there are truly no two alike!

Acknowledgments

I would like to gratefully acknowledge my family, friends, and colleagues who keep me richly supplied with examples, anecdotes, and encouragement. I would also like to express appreciation to my editor, Gwen Weising, for her patience and wise guidance throughout this project. And I especially want to thank Dr. James Dobson and all the Focus on the Family staff. It is an organization that truly makes me feel as though I'm home.

Table of Contents

Chapter One

What Is a Learning Style?

"Here comes the first one!"

The atmosphere in the delivery room was charged with excitement and anticipation. It was a planned C-section, so I was fully awake to witness the arrival of our two sons that April afternoon.

The doctor held up a tiny red baby and whispered, "He's beautiful!" Two minutes later, the doctor held up another baby.

"He looks just like the first one!" a nurse cried.

I recognized them both immediately. On arrival, each boy already seemed to exhibit many of the same behaviors he had demonstrated during the last several months in the womb. The boys and I had started the process of getting to know one another almost from conception, and now I was amazed to see how different these two "identical" babies were from each other. While it will take years to become familiar with each boy's complex nature, their differences were evident from the very beginning.

Friends and acquaintances, gazing at the redheads, often ask "How do you tell them apart?" My standard reply: "Just watch them for a minute—you'll know." If you listen to the way they speak to each other and to you, if you watch the way they interact with people and situations, you will have little doubt that these boys, who share the same birthday, are very much individuals.

When they were still very small, a favorite toy for the twins was a small workbench with hammer and pegs. Robert, our go-for-the-gusto son, took great pleasure in vigorously pounding the pegs. Michael, more analytic by nature, was fascinated by the fact that in the middle of the workbench was a hole just the right size for storing the hammer.

If you are a parent with more than one child, you've already discovered that even children growing up in very similar circumstances and environments can have dramatically *dissimilar* approaches to life. You begin to realize that people are *fundamentally* different. The individual bents that cause each person to be unique, often bring an overwhelming challenge to parents. It is not enough to simply decide how children should be reared and then apply the same techniques to each child. Parents need to get to *know* their children, and *no two will be the same!*

Often, with the very best of intentions, we set out to chart the course and plan the events of our children's lives according to what makes sense to *us*— the way we did it. After all, we are living proof of what works! But what seldom occurs to us is that other people, perhaps even those in our own family, may view the world in an entirely different way than we do. It therefore stands to reason that when we try to teach or communicate with our children and others, they are not all going to benefit from the same approach.

If you're like many busy parents, you may become frustrated when you try to help your child follow directions, do homework, or review for a test. You may be convinced that your child simply isn't *trying* hard enough. The fact is, each of our children perceives the world differently from the way we do. Each child is a unique individual with his or her own natural strengths and preferences. These individual gifts or bents are called *learning styles*.

Although we accept and even cherish each child's uniqueness, it's often difficult to work with the combined variations of all our children when we're also trying to juggle family schedules and the many demands of school and work.

Knowing I was to be the mother of twins, I did a lot of reading. One article had an excellent suggestion for *every* parent. The writer suggested taking at least 15 minutes a day to spend alone with each child. It recommended you choose a safe and fun play area and then let your child show you how he or she prefers to play and interact with you. Short of absolute necessity, you should make no corrections, suggestions, or negative comments. Simply enjoy being with your child. Give as many positive comments as possible, and make some mental notes as to how your child prefers doing things. If you do this consistently with your children, you will be amazed to see how easy it is to identify their different learning styles!

Getting to know each of our children as individuals is an exhausting but rewarding proposition. The busier and more complicated our lives become, the harder it is to remember that each person in our family has a unique and valuable contribution to make from his or her own perspective.

It is my intention to help you discover these different perspectives and to aid you in developing quick, practical ways of helping your child adapt his or her inborn strengths to the varied demands of learning, both in school and throughout the rest of life.

Parents rarely *intentionally* frustrate their children, but intentional or not, it happens. By reading *The Way They Learn*, you can learn to identify many areas of frustration and conflict that can be directly attributed to a mismatch of the child's learning style and the parent's. This is not a deliberate defiance of parental authority by the child. The challenge for parents is to find positive ways of building on their children's natural strengths without sacrificing desired bottom-line outcomes. Believe it or not, it *can* be done!

Another important task for parents is to help their children effectively work with a variety of teachers who will undoubtedly have a number of different teaching styles. After reading this book, you will have gathered some very positive information to share with your children's teachers. Having been a teacher myself, I can tell you that if you will approach both administrators and teachers from a positive perspective, you will be surprised at how open they are to learning about your children's individual styles.

When I first started teaching, I quickly realized that many of my students did not learn the way I did. However, I honestly thought it was just because they didn't know *how*. Surely, if I could teach them to learn *my* way, it would eventually make perfect sense to them.

As a new teacher, I was determined to keep my students excited about school. Since I assumed that they were a lot like me, I decided that boredom was their greatest enemy. I began a one-woman crusade to prevent boredom in my classroom.

The first day of school, after my students left, I rearranged the desks into a new, creative seating plan. I didn't post a formal seating chart, so I was not expecting some of the reactions I got the next day.

"Where do I sit?" several students asked.

"Sit anywhere!" I replied enthusiastically. "The desks make a butterfly today. See the wing tips?"

"Well, where do you *want* us to sit?" they asked uncertainly.

Now I was becoming a bit frustrated. "I don't *care*," I insisted, "just choose a part of the butterfly and enjoy a new seat!"

Now they were walking around the room, peering under the desks.

"Where's the seat I had yesterday?" one student muttered.

That day many of my students notched their desks so they could find the same one the next day. I soon realized that one person's boredom is another person's security. Although I was well-loved and respected for my concern and creativity as a teacher those first years, many students seemed to really struggle with some of my methods. When I later discovered learning styles, I began to accommodate the students many different ways of learning. It was a great relief to know that those students whose styles were so different from my own weren't deliberately trying to annoy me!

This book is just the tip of the iceberg about learning styles. In it, I have highlighted the most practical aspects of five leading research models on the subject. An annotated bibliography is included so that you can continue more in-depth reading or studying. I think you will find it fascinating. For far too long we have had writers and researchers putting people into tight little boxes. But because each person is so complex and unique, no one learning styles model can fully describe what a person *is*. As enlightening as each new chapter of information in this book may be, please remember: Each is only a *piece* of the puzzle. We can recognize and identify patterns of behavior and communication that will become keys for understanding and appreciating style differences. What we dare not do is insist that each person fit neatly into a category.

Even though you will find some potentially invaluable checklists and assessments throughout this book, you will also discover that identifying and understanding individual learning styles is an ongoing journey of observations and impressions. As you read through and begin to use these concepts, keep in mind the following general guidelines:

Observe

Observe patterns of behavior. When you or your child experiences success, what are the circumstances that brought about that success?

Listen

Listen to the way a person communicates. If you only talk to others the way you want them to talk to *you*, you may discover you're speaking a language that is foreign to them. Listening carefully can teach you how you need to talk to them.

Experiment

Experiment with what works and what doesn't. Keep an open mind and remember that even if an approach to learning does not make sense to you, it may work for your children. We do not all learn in the same way.

Focus

Focus on natural strengths, not weaknesses. Unfortunately, it's so much easier to pinpoint areas of weakness that need improvement than to bolster sources of strength. But you can't build much on weaknesses—strengths provide a much better foundation!

Learn

Learn more about learning styles in general. Pay close attention to your children's and your own learning styles in particular.

Everything you discover in this book is only part of the larger picture. There is much more to learn, and that is why I have included an extensive bibliography. While you are reading this book, look for additional pieces of your children's learning style puzzle. Resist the temptation to put labels on your children or anyone else. Don't box them into any one learning style.

Once you begin discovering your natural strengths as well as those of your children, you will probably be relieved to learn that much of their struggle and behavior has more to do with inherent style than with something you failed to do as a parent.

After receiving some learning styles training, one harried home-school mother seemed particularly relieved to find out her young son was "normal." She admitted it had been very difficult to work with him, especially when it came to teaching him music. "Now I understand why," she said. "When I tell him the stems on the notes must be straight, he makes them diagonal, and when I ask him to name the notes, he gives them names like 'Larry.'" This child was not being deliberately difficult. He did not have learning disabilities. He simply applied his own unique perspective to the learning task.

In a Nutshell

Learning how to recognize and appreciate learning styles can help you identify the natural strengths and tendencies each individual possesses. As you read the following chapters, you'll discover some very positive things about yourself as well as your loved ones. This book is only the first step in your odyssey. It usually takes from three to five years of learning about, observing, and using learning styles information before it becomes second nature. Be patient with yourself, and don't worry about trying to formally identify people according to a particular learning style label.

Dr. Holland London, a seasoned clergyman and powerful communicator, recently spoke at a gathering I attended. In his inimitable way, he spoke on a variety of subjects in a very short time with wit and wisdom. At one point he paused and leaned closer to the microphone. "People often ask me why I take so many detours when I speak. I just tell them it's because those I'm trying to reach don't live on the highway."

As a parent and an educator, I sat there thinking about how hard we try to get children to move onto the highway so that we don't have to put up with the inconvenience of detours.

Perhaps instead of spending so much time and effort trying to convince our children to move onto the path we've designed, we could encourage them to get to their destination by allowing them a few minor detours. Who knows? We may even discover some places *we'd* like to travel off the beaten path!

Chapter Two

What Style Are You?

Послушайте меня

*A Russian phrase meaning
"Listen to me!"*

If I spoke to you in Russian but you didn't know the Russian language, you wouldn't understand me. If I noticed your bewildered expression, I might slow down and repeat my Russian phrase more clearly and in a louder tone. But despite my best efforts, no matter how many times I repeated it, how well I articulated it, or how loudly I spoke it, as long as I continued to speak Russian, the chances are pretty remote that you would understand what I was saying.

How often have you heard yourself saying to your children: "How many times do I have to *tell* you this?" or "What did I just *say*? Didn't you hear what I *just said*?" The fact is, they probably did hear the words you said but didn't understand what you meant. Each of us takes in information in a different way, and because our learning styles are so diverse, we may as well be trying to communicate with each other in two languages.

Early in our relationship, my husband and I frequently struggled to get our point across to one another. One day in frustration he said, "I'm just talking to *you* the way I want you to talk to *me*." He paused and then added, "And I guess maybe you're doing the same thing."

For the first time, we both realized that the golden rule, "Do unto others as you'd have them do unto you," doesn't always work when trying to communicate. If we only talk to people in the way we prefer they talk back to us, and they are busy doing the same thing, chances are good that no one is truly listening: We haven't reached a common level of communication.

THE GREGORC MODEL OF LEARNING STYLES

One of the most effective models for understanding learning style differences comes from the research of Dr. Anthony F. Gregorc. His model provides invaluable insights into how our minds perceive and understand information. Let's take a careful look at it.

Two Points of View

Perception: *The way we take in information.*

We know people are not all alike. What we don't always realize is that each of us tends to view the world in a way that makes the most sense to us as individuals. The way in which we view the world is called our *perception*. Perceptions shape what we think, how we make decisions, and how we define what's important to us. Our individual perceptions also determine our natural learning strengths, or *learning styles*.

There are two perceptual qualities that each mind possesses. They are **concrete** perception and **abstract** perception.

Concrete

This quality lets us register information directly through our five senses: sight, smell, touch, taste, and hearing. When we are using our *concrete* abilities, we are dealing with what is here and now—the tangible, the obvious. We are not looking for hidden meanings or trying to make relationships between ideas or concepts. The key phrase simply stated is **"It is what it is."**

Abstract This quality allows us to visualize, to conceive ideas, to understand or believe what we can't actually see. When we are using this *abstract* quality, we are using our intuition, our intellect, our imagination: We are looking beyond what *is* to the more subtle implications. The key phrase for the abstract is **"It's not always what it seems."**

Although everyone uses *both* concrete and abstract perceptual abilities every day, each person is more *comfortable* using one over the other. This becomes his or her dominant ability. For example, the person whose natural strength is *concrete* may prefer to listen in a direct, literal, no-nonsense manner. The person whose natural strength is *abstract* may often pick up the more subtle cues from others as they communicate.

My husband was driving on a busy Los Angeles freeway when I noticed a unique billboard and said to him, "John, look at that billboard!" John turned and looked. He looked and looked, and pretty soon we were driving into someone else's lane of traffic. Horns were honking; people were shouting.

I turned to him. "John, watch where you're driving, for heaven's sake!"

He replied calmly, "Cindy, you told me to *look* at the billboard. Did you mean *glance*?"

I was exasperated. "Wouldn't you *assume* that?"

He shook his head. "I assume nothing. You said look and I looked. The billboard hadn't done anything yet, and you didn't tell me what to look *for*."

John, using concrete perceptions, took what I said at face value. It never occurred to me that he would take it quite so literally. It takes the abstract perceptual ability to "read between the lines."

Using What We Know

Ordering: *The way we use the information we perceive.*

Once we've taken the information in, we all use two methods of ordering what we know. According to Gregorc, the two ordering abilities are sequential and random.

Sequential

A sequential method of ordering allows our minds to organize information in a linear, step-by-step manner. When using *sequential* ability, we are following a logical train of thought, a conventional approach to dealing with information. Those who have strong sequential ordering abilities may prefer to have a plan and follow it, rather than relying on impulse. Their key phrase is "Follow the steps."

Random

Random ordering lets our minds organize information by chunks and with no particular sequence. When we are using our *random* ability, we may often be able to skip steps in a procedure and still produce the desired result. We might even start in the middle or begin at the end and work backwards. Those with a strong random way of ordering information may seem impulsive or more spontaneous. It appears as if they do not *have* a plan. Their key phrase is "Just get it done!"

Learning Styles

The way in which we view the world is called our . . .

Perception

We perceive in two ways . . .

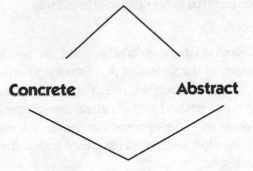

Concrete   **Abstract**

The way we use the information we perceive is called . . .

Ordering

We order in two ways . . .

Sequential   **Random**

At a recent training workshop attended primarily by accountants and data processors, the participants were asked how many balanced their checkbooks monthly. The majority, of course, were very careful to balance to the penny.

One man raised his hand and said, "I took the checkbook away from my wife." As the group frowned, he quickly explained. "We have checks that are a series of pictures. My wife was giving her checks out according to which *picture* she thought the person would like best. She thought as long as all the numbers were used, it wouldn't matter whether or not they were in order. So, she'd be at a fish market and say, 'Wait a minute, I think I have a picture of a fish on one of these!' "

What was considered essential to this detail-oriented, sequential accountant hadn't even occurred to his random-oriented wife.

Four Combinations

When we take all of Gregorc's definitions and put them together, we get four combinations of the strongest perceptual and ordering abilities. Remember, no individual is only *one* style. Each of us has a dominant style or styles that give us a unique blend of natural strengths and abilities.

From perception and ordering come four dominant learning styles. The following charts list some words most often used to describe those who are dominant in each style.

Four Combinations

Concrete Sequential (CS)

hardworking

conventional

accurate

stable

dependable

consistent

factual

organized

Abstract Sequential (AS)

analytic

objective

knowledgeable

thorough

structured

logical

deliberate

systematic

Abstract Random (AR)

sensitive

compassionate

perceptive

imaginative

idealistic

sentimental

spontaneous

flexible

Concrete Random (CR)

quick

intuitive

curious

realistic

creative

innovative

instinctive

adventurous

By learning some of the common characteristics of each of these combinations (CS, AS, AR, CR), we can recognize and value what we like to do best and what comes naturally for us. We can also learn to identify and improve characteristics that we avoid because we do not understand them well.

We, as parents, must first recognize our *own* natural learning styles. As we recognize how *we* learn new information, we can better understand what comes naturally to us and to our children, and can identify the differences between parents and children that cause frustration and misunderstanding.

The following checklist is a quick, informal method of identifying some of our own learning style characteristics. If you would like to do a formal assessment of your style, you will want to order *The Gregorc Adult Style Delineator*,[1] available directly from Dr. Gregorc. Once again, keep in mind that all of us are combinations of these four learning styles. No person will fit neatly into any one category.

Dominant Learning Style Characteristics

Describe what you prefer *most of the time*. Place a check mark beside every phrase under each section that describes your preferences. Check as many as you feel *strongly* describe you.

Dominant Concrete Sequential (CS)

I almost *always*:

___prefer doing things the same way

___work best with people who won't hesitate to take immediate action

___am more interested in obvious facts than in finding hidden meanings

___prefer a neat and orderly environment

___ask first "How do I do it?"

Total:____

Dominant Abstract Sequential (AS)

I almost *always*:

___want as much information as possible before making a decision

___need enough time to do a thorough job

___prefer to get directions in writing

___am interested in where a person got the facts

___ask "Where do I find more information?"

Total:____

Dominant Abstract Random (AR)

I almost *always*:

___prefer to check with others before making final decisions

___try to be sensitive to other people's feelings

___work well with others

___am not bothered by a cluttered environment

___ask the advice of others when in doubt

Total:____

Dominant Concrete Random (CR)

I almost *always*:

___solve problems creatively

___act on the spur of the moment

___work best with those who can keep up

___like frequent changes in the environment

___prefer to learn only what's necessary to know

Total:____

Based on the work of Anthony F. Gregorc, Ph.D. Adapted by Cynthia Ulrich Tobias, M.Ed.
(Do not reproduce without written permission)

Now that you have an idea what your dominant learning style might be, here's a quick overview and comparison of the four styles on some key issues.

What Do They Do Best?

Dominant Concrete Sequential (CS)
Their Key Word: *Facts*

- apply ideas in a practical way
- organize
- fine-tune ideas to make them more efficient, economical, etc.
- produce concrete products from abstract ideas
- work well within time limits

Dominant Abstract Sequential (AS)
Their Key Words: *Underlying Principles*

- gather data before making decisions
- analyze ideas
- research
- provide logical sequence
- use facts to prove or disprove theories
- analyze the means to achieve a goal

Dominant Abstract Random (AR)
Their Key Words: *Personal Relevance*

- listen sincerely to others
- understand feelings and emotions
- focus on themes and ideas
- bring harmony to group situations
- have good rapport with almost anybody
- recognize the emotional needs of others

Dominant Concrete Random (CR)
Their Key Words: *Compelling Reasons*

- inspire others to take action
- see many options and solutions
- contribute unusual and creative ideas
- visualize the future
- often find a different way to do things
- accept many types of people
- think fast on their feet
- take risks

What Makes the Most Sense to Them?

Dominant Concrete Sequential (CS)

- working systematically, step by step
- paying close attention to details
- having a schedule to follow
- using literal interpretations
- knowing what's expected of them
- establishing routines, and ways of doing things

Dominant Abstract Sequential (AS)

- using exact, well-researched information
- learning more by watching than doing
- using logical reasoning
- needing a teacher who is an expert on the subject
- living in the world of abstract ideas
- working through an issue thoroughly

Dominant Abstract Random (AR)

- personalizing learning
- having broad, general principles
- maintaining friendly relationships with everyone whenever possible
- participating enthusiastically in projects they believe in
- emphasizing high morale
- deciding with the heart, not the head

Dominant Concrete Random (CR)

- using insight and instinct to solve problems
- working with general time frames rather than specific deadlines
- developing and testing many solutions
- using real-life experiences to learn
- trying something themselves rather than taking your word for it

What's Hard For Them?

Dominant Concrete Sequential (CS)

- working in groups
- discussion with no specific point
- working in an disorganized environment
- following incomplete or unclear directions
- working with abstract ideas
- demands to "use your imagination"
- questions with no right or wrong answers

Dominant Abstract Sequential (AS)

- no time to deal with a subject thoroughly
- repeating the same tasks over
- lots of specific rules and regulations
- "sentimental" thinking
- expressing their emotions
- being diplomatic when convincing someone else of their point of view
- not monopolizing a conversation about a subject that interests them

Dominant Abstract Random (AR)

- having to explain or justify feelings
- competition
- working with unfriendly people
- giving exact details
- accepting even positive criticism
- focusing on one thing at a time

Dominant Concrete Random (CR)

- restrictions and limitations
- formal reports
- routines
- re-doing anything once it's done
- keeping detailed records
- showing how they got an answer
- choosing only one answer
- having no options

What Questions Do They Ask When Learning?

Dominant Concrete Sequential (CS)

- What facts do I need?
- How do I do it?
- What should it look like?
- When is it due?

Dominant Abstract Sequential (AS)

- How do I know this is true?
- Have we considered all the possibilities?
- What will we need to accomplish this?

Dominant Abstract Random (AR)

- What does this have to do with me?
- How can I make a difference?

Dominant Concrete Random (CR)

- How much of this is really necessary?

In a Nutshell

Just because your children aren't responding to you doesn't always mean they aren't listening. It could be that the difference in your perspectives is so great that you sometimes might as well be living in different countries and speaking different languages. Learning to listen to *how* something is said instead of just the *words* that are said can help everyone communicate more effectively. It can literally make a world of difference!

Chapter Three

The Dominant
Concrete Sequential (CS)
Learning Style

It was board meeting night for the local church. For some reason, those who attended that particular meeting preferred a more random style of learning and communicating. Missing from the meeting were the Concrete Sequentials, those who approach tasks in a step-by-step manner. Since there was a quorum, the randoms decided to go ahead with the meeting.

The main item on the agenda was promotion of the upcoming rally. "Hey!" someone said excitedly, "I've got a great idea!" (A phrase, by the way, that strikes dread into most CS hearts!) "What if we bought 1,000 balloons and filled them with helium? We could put a notice about the rally inside each balloon and release them into the sky. They would come down all over the area, and people would find out about the event." All the other randoms thought that was a wonderful idea, and later that week one of them went out and bought the balloons.

Before the actual launching of the event, however, there was one more board meeting and the CS members showed up that night. The randoms enthusiastically shared their plan, and the CSs politely listened. At the end, one CS raised his hand. "Do you know how far helium balloons *go* before they come down?" he asked.

The randoms looked a bit uncomfortable. "Well, no," one admitted. The CS replied, "They've been known to go as far as 200 or 300 miles. I don't think people on the other side of the mountains will come."

"Oh, yeah, we didn't think of that," a random said.

Another CS raised her hand. "Do you know how *long* helium balloons stay in the air before they come down?" she inquired.

"No." A random admitted, now a bit sheepish.

She continued. "They've been known to stay up as long as two or three months. The rally will be over."

And the randoms said quietly, "Oh, yeah, you're right."

The box of 1,000 balloons still sits, unused, under an office desk. But the board members learned a valuable lesson. In times past, the randoms had sometimes thought that the CSs were just shooting down good ideas and critically picking apart visionary plans. Now they realized that the CSs' contributions were invaluable. These days at that church's board meetings, it's not unusual to hear someone say: "Wait! We can't start without the CSs!"

THE DOMINANT CONCRETE SEQUENTIAL ADULT

When presented with an abstract idea, Concrete Sequentials have a special talent for seeing the practical side of an issue. They have a knack for knowing how to get the most productive use out of any item or plan—for streamlining and making everything work more efficiently. Their natural ability to think in a linear manner makes them people who can actually put together those "ready-to-assemble" products by following the step-by-step instructions.

A CS lives life in a fairly straightforward manner. Verbal communication sometimes comes across as clipped and bossy. The CS attitude is "If it needs to be done, you do it," and "If it needs to be said, you say it." The CSs are no-nonsense communicators, saying what they mean and meaning what they say. They don't usually pick up on subtle clues or hidden meanings. They prefer you tell them exactly what it is you want them to do.

Although my husband is dominantly Abstract Sequential, he is also very CS. I learned long ago that when he uses his CS style, he needs more than hints to fulfill my wish list for gifts on special occasions. On our first Christmas together, he really built up his "big gift" to me. "It's red," he said, "something you'd never buy for yourself, and it's too big to fit under the tree." On Christmas Day, I found my gift sitting in the carport. It was a bright, shiny red . . . lawnmower! After a few more Christmases of receiving jumper cables, blenders, and shower curtains, I finally came to grips with the fact that he could not read my mind. He would keep telling me that he truly wanted to make me happy—but I needed to *tell* him what would *make* me happy. Although he's getting better at remembering what I like, he's absolutely thrilled when I just make him a list of exactly what I want.

Giving practical gifts is only one way dominant CSs demonstrate their ability for being down-to-earth and realistic. Because of their hands-on sequential nature, CSs are very good at making and keeping schedules and organizing and maintaining systems. List-making comes naturally, and some extreme CSs even admit to being so dependent on a list that if they do something *not* on the list they *add* it so they can have the satisfaction of crossing it off. CSs are often the ones taking up the slack, picking up the pieces, cleaning up the messes, and putting away the leftovers. CSs would rather do it themselves than leave it undone, but if they do it, they do not suffer silently! Those who live with CSs may find notes reminding them of their responsibilities, or they may receive quick lectures designed to leave them feeling at least a *little* guilty.

THE DOMINANT CONCRETE SEQUENTIAL PARENT

The bleary-eyed couple was almost an hour late to the Saturday morning parenting workshop. The woman was very apologetic. "I'm afraid we overslept. We rented the three most *boring* movies last night," she explained. "It took us until almost 2 A.M. to finish watching them."

When I asked why they had subjected themselves to such an endlessly boring evening, she looked surprised. "Why, we *paid* to watch the movies. We *started* them. *We couldn't just quit in the middle!*"

Dominant CSs have a definite sense of order and responsibility, and they need to have a beginning, a middle, *and* an end. When dealing with their children, it is common for CS parents to:

- Communicate with their children in a literal, specific manner and expect the same in return.
- Believe that a yes or no question deserves a yes or no response, not a lengthy explanation.
- Expect instruction to be followed without question or procrastination.
- Clearly lay out the rules children are expected to follow, as well as the consequences for disobedience. Both are specific and consistent.
- Become frustrated when they have to say things more than once.
- Become exasperated at the child who seems to choose the "hard way" to do what the CS sees as a simple task.

CS parents almost always have high expectations when it comes to their children's behavior and academic success. After all, the CS parent probably had little trouble adapting to the traditional learning methods most schools use, since those methods tend to be concrete and sequential. If a child is struggling, the CS parent may often believe it is because that child is simply not trying hard enough.

CS parents are not likely to accept excuses like "It's too hard," "I don't like it," or "I just don't get it!" Part of the CS nature is to simply do what needs to be done, whether or not you *feel* like it. Duty and obligation play a big part in their own lives, and they expect their children to respond in the same way.

When it comes to discipline, the CS parent expects the child to do what he's told or suffer the consequences. In the CS parent's mind, the *threat* of punishment should be enough to prevent the bad behavior. When children don't do what they're told the first time, a favorite CS method for getting quick action is the "countdown."

Although the countdown works for many children, it does not work for all. For example, my mom would say to my sister, "Sandee, I want you here by the time I count to three! One . . . two . . . " and Sandee was *there*.

I, on the other hand, was not so compliant. My strong-willed nature compelled me to ride out the threat. Mom would start counting. "One . . . two . . . two-and-a-half . . . two-and-three-quarters . . . two-and-seven-eighths. . . ." I often called her bluff, just to see what would happen. Inevitably, I would experience the consequences!

Here is another classic example of style contrast. A CS parent frowns disapprovingly at the strong-willed, Concrete Random child who is contemplating standing on the coffee table and warns, "If you stand on that table, I'll spank you." The CR child pauses a moment, then shrugs and says, "OK, go ahead and spank me. How hard could it be? How long could it last? It's worth it."

To CS parents, the mere threat of a spanking would have been sufficient. It's hard for them to understand a child who would rather be punished than be pressured into obeying.

On the other hand, for a CS child, the CS parent's methods and approach make sense almost automatically. After all, they understand how each other's minds work. The CS child finds it comforting to know what to expect, and there is a sense of security about the consistency of routine and schedule. For the more random child, however, the CS parent's approach often seems dictatorial and rigid. Because a random person's perspective is so drastically different from a sequential's, trying to understand each other's point of view may literally be like listening to a foreign language.

THE DOMINANT CONCRETE SEQUENTIAL CHILD

Kelli was a bright and conscientious third grader. The class that caused her the most difficulty was history. One evening she had just read the chapter on Georgia, and she was answering the questions at the end. The first question was "What are Savannah, Georgia's, natural resources?" Kelli was stumped. She reread the entire chapter but could not find those two words, *natural resources*. As she was becoming more and more frustrated, her dad sat down with her. "What's the problem, Kelli?" he asked.

"I can't find *natural resources* anywhere," Kelli sighed. Her dad then defined the term and gave her one or two examples. Suddenly, a light went on for Kelli. This time as she went back through the chapter, she quickly picked them out. Because of her dominant CS style, she had easily remembered specific details. However, she had to be taught to recognize abstract concepts. Like their parental counterparts, CS children are very good at dealing with facts, but they have to work at seeing the abstract, bigger picture.

Some common characteristics of Dominant Concrete Sequential children are:

- They are usually very organized, specific, and conscientious.
- They may ask repeatedly for clarification or more detailed instructions because of their need to be sure they are doing things right.
- They are almost always more secure when there is a pattern to follow, model to copy, or someone to go first and show them how it's done.
- In getting CS children to do their chores, learn responsibility, and practice acceptable behaviors, they respond best to tangible rewards and hands-on methods. Often a schedule or checklist on the refrigerator is a great motivator for young CS children. Stars, stickers, and even cash are all effective rewards for a job well done.
- Consistency is especially important, and CS children may frequently have to remind their more random parents of a promise or a missed step in the routine. It may not even occur to the random parent to *create* a checklist, much less keep it up to date!
- CS children will generally take parents at their word. Since CSs tend to be very literal in their communication, more abstract parents may find their instructions misunderstood because they assumed their CS children understood what was *meant*, not just what was *said*.

A young mother was concerned when her five-year-old daughter came home from the first day of kindergarten absolutely exhausted. "Why are you so tired?" Mom asked.

The new kindergartner replied breathlessly, "Oh, Mom, I practically *ran* all day long!"

"Why did you run so much?"

The child answered very seriously. "Well, the teacher said 'When you're on the sidewalk, *walk*; when you're on the grass, *run*.' I was on the grass a *lot*, so I just had to keep running." This mother got pretty clear signals about how strong the CS characteristics are in her child!

Ten-year-old Tracy is a very conscientious, literal CS child and has been from the very beginning. During a recent visit to a shopping mall, she asked a question that had evidently been on her mind for awhile. "Why do those big trash cans say 'THANK YOU' on the flap?"

Her mother patiently explained, "It's to thank people who put their trash in there."

Tracy nodded her understanding but persisted. "But not everyone *puts* their trash in there."

Her mother waved her hand in dismissal. "Well, it just thanks the people who do."

Tracy frowned and pronounced her CS opinion. "Then it should say, 'THANK YOU *IF* YOU PUT YOUR TRASH IN HERE.'"

Parents of children like Tracy can help their CS offspring capitalize on this gift for literal interpretation by first understanding for themselves and then pointing out to the child the benefits of being a CS. For example, CSs catch a lot of mistakes because they look at everything so literally! When CS children feel reassured about the value of their natural communication strengths, it becomes easier to encourage them to stretch and look *beyond* their style.

WHAT ABOUT STRESS?

When it comes to what causes and relieves stress, the dominant CS parents and children have a lot in common.

The Dominant Concrete Sequential usually thrives with

organization	predictability	schedules
routines	tangible rewards	literal language

The Dominant Concrete Sequential is often stressed by

too much to do	not knowing expectations
not knowing where to begin	vague or general directions
no clean, quiet places	not seeing an example

You can frequently lessen the stress by

giving specific time and space for quiet, uninterrupted work
asking what you can do to help
providing a concrete example of what is expected
practicing "what if" scenarios to prepare for the unexpected

CONCRETE SEQUENTIAL

What People with Other Styles Admire Most About CSs

organization
attention to detail
completion of tasks
productivity
stability and dependability

Negative Perception By People with Other Styles

perfectionists
things often seem more important than people
tunnel-vision
lack of adaptibility
impatient

Ten Commandments for Getting Along with a CS

Thou shalt:
be consistent
be organized
practice common sense
pull your own weight
remember I have feelings, too
give advance notice so I can prepare myself
follow instructions
tell me what you want
take responsibility for your actions
not deal in generalities

In a Nutshell

Dominant Concrete Sequentials contribute a great deal to their families and to society with their natural bent toward organization, predictability, literal communication, and the ability to follow and give step-by-step instructions. Their greatest creativity may show up when they are fine-tuning and improving someone else's original idea. They provide a stable, predictable backdrop in the lives of those who may not even realize how much they count on having them be there. Their consistency and reliability often make them more valuable than some randoms would like to admit. Remember that everyone has at least *some* of the CS learning style in them. Just because it's not your dominant style doesn't mean you can't use it at least briefly when you need to. The more you learn to recognize CS strengths, the more you will appreciate those who come by them naturally!

Chapter Four

The Dominant
Abstract Sequential (AS)
Learning Style

It was still early in their marriage when a young couple discovered they needed to replace one of their cars. The young wife, acting in her typically random fashion, said enthusiastically, "Let's go to the car lot and look around!" Her husband, a Dominant Abstract Sequential, looked at her incredulously. "We don't even know what we're *looking* for," he stated. She shrugged. "Won't we know when we see it?"

Three weeks later, after they had listed critical attributes, researched *Consumer Reports*, charted interest rates and lease options, and had driven the top 10 cars twice, she realized her car buying days would never be the same as they were before marriage. Although her AS husband took all the *romance* out of car shopping, they *did* make a significantly more economical choice. Now if he would just quit second-guessing himself on whether or not they had bought at exactly the right *time*!

THE DOMINANT ABSTRACT SEQUENTIAL ADULT

When it comes to making decisions, the dominantly AS person feels compelled to explore virtually all the options. As a matter of fact, the information-gathering process is so important to ASs, that they don't do much of *anything* without a great deal of deliberation and thought. ASs are gifted with a natural sense of logic and reason. They evaluate almost everything, from major life decisions and purchases to a simple lunch choice on a restaurant menu.

What is especially unique about the AS evaluation process is that the analysis does not stop even after the final decision has been made. Although the process is done less actively, ASs admit that they never really stop looking to make sure there isn't a better option.

If an item has already been purchased and the AS later finds a better deal, there are, for the AS, really only two choices. If it's not too late, the item is exchanged. If it *is* too late, ASs may kick themselves for years, and there's almost nothing you can do to lessen the remorse.

Even though this may sound extreme, I've been told by several ASs that their penchant for finding the absolute best bargain even extends to the gifts they receive. As they are opening their gifts, the most dominant of them can't resist calculating how they could get *twice* the merchandise for the exchange value of the gift if they just waited for the right sale.

Analysis comes naturally to ASs, and most believe there can *never* really be enough information. They seem to be on a continual search for knowledge. There aren't enough hours in each day for ASs to do the research they feel needs to be done.

Since most ASs assume that everyone has the same need they do for extensive information, you may frequently get very long answers to short questions. It's difficult for ASs not to monopolize the conversation when it's a topic that interests them. And even though you may be finished listening, they may not pick up on your impatience.

The need for analysis and objectivity carries over into the more personal aspects of the AS's life. Although ASs may experience as much emotion as the next person, they believe that their emotions should be justified by facts. For example, I'm told by many ASs that falling in love is a difficult situation when it comes to applying principles of logic and reason. Most ASs may revel in the euphoric emotion of love, but they rarely make a serious commitment until they are certain there are solid and reliable facts to back up their emotional involvement. ASs will rarely share what they are feeling until they have a handle on *why* they are feeling the way they do. By the same token, they expect you to be able to justify *your* emotions.

I learned some important lessons about ASs early in my relationship with the AS man who is now my husband. We had only been dating about three months when we had a pretty serious argument. I was so upset when we parted that I went right home and poured my jumbled thoughts out on paper, not sure if I actually dared to send the letter to John. After some soul searching, I went ahead and mailed it.

A day or so later, John called me, and asked if he could take me to lunch to discuss my letter. He picked me up, and while we were sitting in the car, he took out my heartfelt, soul-baring epistle. He had rewritten it in outline form—Roman numeral I, II, III; subhead A, B, C. I was too horrified to speak! He sensed my dismay and quickly explained. "Cindy, I love you. What you wrote obviously meant a lot to you. If I were to just answer you off the top of my head, I might well miss the points that were most important to you. So I put this in a format where I could be sure all your concerns were addressed."

How could I argue with that? His meticulous approach that at first seemed to be so cold and calculating was actually motivated by the same love and tenderness that had caused me to randomly spill my thoughts on paper.

THE DOMINANT ABSTRACT SEQUENTIAL PARENT

I'll never forget one morning when Robert, one of our 18-month-old sons, had been fussing and crying for hours, and we could find no solution for his tears. Finally in frustration, John said, "Rob! For heaven's sake, just *articulate* what it is you *want!*"

AS parents insist that their children demonstrate at least some semblance of logical thought and analysis. Because of a naturally intellectual bent, ASs sometimes forget they are dealing with young children and not their own peers. AS parents tend to have high expectations for their offspring. Remember, ASs believe in thorough deliberation and complete analysis of virtually every situation. A simple request from a child like "Could I have a puppy?" may very well bring about more trouble than that child thinks it's worth! The AS parent will likely respond with questions like, "What kind of puppy? Where will you keep it? What will you feed it? How will you keep it groomed? How much will the upkeep cost?" ASs may even require that their children keep detailed records or present a well-thought-out written request in the first place.

It is especially important to AS parents that their children learn to think logically. ASs feel compelled to look beyond the obvious and find the underlying principle. It is this understanding of the "moral of the story" that often creates the need for an AS parent to be sure the child has "learned his lesson." ASs have a strong need for closure, and they often find themselves asking their child, "Now, what have you learned from this?" A child with a random style may create a great deal of frustration for the AS parent, because it seems almost impossible to direct that dominantly random mind into a structured analysis of circumstances or problems.

I recently heard an excellent suggestion from a visiting professor. She said her AS husband was very fond of lecturing their impatient and impetuous random teenage daughter. The girl hated the long, drawn out lectures, and her father was very annoyed by her apparent lack of attention. After several unsuccessful encounters, they came up with a unique agreement. When the father began his lecture, his daughter could stop him at any time during the lecture and state what she thought the point was that he was trying to make. If she got it right, he had to abort the rest of the lecture. If she missed the point he was allowed to continue until she hit upon the actual point he was making. Now he knew she was listening, and she knew she would not need to endure a prolonged explanation of a point he had already driven home.

This is the kind of compromise that can help AS parents come to terms with children who do not share their drive to analyze, verbalize, and philosophize.

THE DOMINANT ABSTRACT SEQUENTIAL CHILD

A frustrated home-school mom struggled with her AS first grader as she tried to teach him to read. Somehow Jimmy had gotten the idea that he should already *know* how to read. Because he felt he was starting at a disadvantage, he simply avoided his reading lessons altogether. After reading about learning styles and discovering that Jimmy's AS traits called for more distance and objectivity, his mother hit upon a unique solution. She took Jimmy to the store and told him he could choose any puppet that appealed to him. He selected Molasses the Moose. When they got the puppet home, mother and child began to teach Molasses to read. Now there was objective distance, and there was no longer a stigma in Jimmy's mind about learning the basics. This AS child rapidly learned while teaching Molasses, all the while making sure that his moose paid close attention and worked very diligently.

Dominant Abstract Sequential children are usually as systematic and deliberate as their parental counterparts. These children almost always need more time to complete tasks to their satisfaction. Although they may appear to be slow, it is often a case of being thorough. Parents of AS children express amazement when the child would rather not do an assignment or project at *all* if there is not time to do it *completely*. Frequently, AS children can have a homework assignment almost completely finished, but if told to "just turn in what you have," they will turn in nothing.

It is common for AS children to appear quieter and more withdrawn. Their minds are working through the analytic and evaluative process, and it's not likely they will verbalize what they are thinking until they understand it.

One extroverted mother became very worried about her uncommunicative AS daughter, Allison. The young girl would spend hours alone in her room, thinking and reading. She would rarely contribute verbally to family or classroom discussions. Allison's written assignments, however, were almost always superb. Allison's mother attended one of my workshops on learning styles and discovered her daughter's AS strengths. After coming to understand her daughter's approach, this normally outspoken mother was able to appreciate the depth of insight Allison possessed. Once she let her AS daughter work in solitude without pressure, she discovered Allison began to be more comfortable verbalizing how she felt.

AS children have a gift of objectivity that begins to show up at a very early age, and they are often uncomfortable with tasks or assignments that seem too personal. It is difficult for the AS to share emotions, especially if the emotions cannot be explained logically or categorized efficiently. Even "show and tell" at school can be painful if the AS is forced to reveal something that seems to intrude upon their privacy. Parents can often help their AS children deal with their discomfort if they encourage their AS child to analyze *why* this particular assignment is important.

WHAT ABOUT STRESS?

When it comes to what causes and relieves stress, the dominant AS parent and child have a lot in common.

The Dominant Abstract Sequential usually thrives with

organization	credible sources of information
logical outcomes	opportunities for analysis
plenty of time to work	appreciation for their input

The Dominant Abstract Sequential is often stressed by

being rushed through anything
unreasonable deadlines
not having hard questions answered
abiding by sentimental decisions
being asked to express emotions or feelings

You can frequently lessen the stress by

providing additional time to complete tasks
giving lots of space and quiet time to work
putting as much as possible in writing
appreciating the less emotional aspects of a situation

ABSTRACT SEQUENTIAL

What People with Other Styles Admire Most About ASs

analyze before making a decision
ability to conceptualize an idea
intellect
precision
ready knowledge

Negative Perceptions by People with Other Styles

aloofness
not in touch with reality
have to have an explanation for everything
highly opinionated
perceive things in numbers, not effort

Ten Commandments for Getting Along with an AS

Thou shalt:

have specific goals when dealing with me

use logic and reason

listen to what I have to say

give me a job, leave me alone, and let me do it

be complete and thorough

be deliberate

keep issues factual

give me time to research projects for the best approach

make certain I understand the purpose of the project

don't expect immediate response—I need time to think
        and research

In a Nutshell

The dominant AS learner is in the minority among the general population. The views of the strong AS will not always make sense to or even be welcomed by those who do not share the same devotion to logic and objectivity. Although it may seem that the AS has an entirely too serious and methodical perspective on life, there is also a warm and loving side that can sometimes be overlooked by those who don't recognize or value the AS's approach. Once again, we all have at least a little of every learning style. Even if your AS tendencies are virtually hidden, learning how to access this part of your style can definitely be a benefit!

Chapter Five

The Dominant
Abstract Random(AR)
Learning Style

The suspect in the crime sat alone in the interrogation room. Officer Baker, one of the department's best by-the-book cops, stormed out in frustration. "He won't talk! I tried every method we were ever taught, and the guy won't budge."

Detective Frye smiled and said, "Let me talk to him."

"I'm telling you," Baker said angrily, "I've tried it all."

Detective Frye had been in the room less than five minutes when Baker, watching the suspect through the one-way mirror, stared in disbelief. The suspect's head was in his hands, and he was sobbing. Detective Frye had turned on the recorder, and the full confession took less than an hour.

"What did you do?" Baker asked when Frye came out.

Detective Frye shrugged. "I just talked to him."

THE DOMINANT ABSTRACT RANDOM ADULT

During my time as a police officer, I noticed that dominant sequential detectives and police officers had a particularly frustrating time dealing with unpredictable or uncooperative people. In the police academy we were taught how to interrogate a suspect, interview a victim, and solicit information from a witness. There are certain procedures to follow. So, when a sequential officer follows procedure to the letter and those tried-and-true methods fail to work, he is often at a loss. That's what happened in the story above. Officer Baker, a CS, could not understand how Detective Frye, an Abstract Random could come over, speak a couple sentences, and cause the suspect to pour out his heart. In many cases, the technique simply isn't something one could learn from a book.

The AR has a sixth sense when it comes to reading people or understanding what others need without anyone verbalizing those needs aloud. Nonverbal cues that may completely escape the more sequential person can speak volumes to the AR.

Because ARs place so much trust in intuition, their instincts become more and more accurate over the years. Unfortunately, it does not seem to get any easier for ARs to explain *how* they know what they know if they did not use sequential abilities in arriving at conclusions.

The Dominant Abstract Random person believes there is more to life than cold hard facts or endless details. People are more important than things, and life is too short to get caught up in conflict or uncomfortable situations. They often find themselves the peacemakers, sometimes at their own expense. It is difficult for ARs to work in situations where there is unhappiness or disharmony. For many ARs, it seems as though they are constantly having to smooth over rough words said by someone else, or apologize for the actions of a thoughtless colleague or family member.

It is especially important for ARs to feel included. Before making a decision, they almost always seek the input of trusted friends and family. ARs are at their best when they are part of a team process. Soliciting opinions from those around them helps them maintain a cooperative life-style.

Although my dominant style is Concrete Random, my AR preferences are very strong. I noticed how heavily I relied on it early in my dating relationship with my very sequential husband. We experienced a conflict common to many couples.

John would ask, "Do you want to go out for dinner?"

"Yes," I would reply enthusiastically.

"Where would you like to go?" he would query.

Not wanting to make an unpopular choice, I would hedge. "I don't know, what do *you* feel like eating?"

He would shrug. "It doesn't matter. Just choose a restaurant."

Not actually *believing* that it didn't matter, I would keep after him until he became impatient with me. Why couldn't I just make a *decision*? I would feel hurt. Didn't he realize it was because I valued his opinion? Of course, by the time we finally *did* get to a restaurant, we were too irritated with each other to enjoy our dinner.

Eventually we both realized what the other one needed, so John then designed an almost foolproof method for avoiding the conflict. Now when the question of where to go for dinner comes up, he says: "Chinese, Mexican, or American?" He chooses three cuisines he would be equally happy eating.

"Chinese," I say.

He then suggests three Chinese restaurants he finds equally appealing. I choose one of those three, and we're off, usually in less than a minute. I get the necessary input, he gets a quick decision, and we both enjoy our evening!

What may sometimes seem to others to be a lack of conviction or inability to make up their minds, is often simply the ARs' efforts to make sure that everyone involved in the process gets what he or she needs. In reality, ARs often possess the strongest convictions of all, and once they have chosen a battlefield, no one is more committed to the end result.

THE ABSTRACT RANDOM PARENT

The room was happily chaotic, with piles of papers, crumpled food wrappers, and freshly laundered clothes waiting to be folded. Almost hidden on the desk was a lovingly framed sign declaring a cheerful, AR motto: A tidy house is the sign of a misspent life!

Although ARs can keep house as well as any sequential, housekeeping is not a high priority if there are personal needs to fulfill. By nature, ARs are somewhat unstructured and free-flowing, and they often struggle when it comes to keeping a consistent schedule or detailed routine. Dominantly AR parents are warm, nurturing, and full of praise and reassurance for their children. When it comes to dealing with a more sequential child, AR parents can be perceived as inconsistent, even though it may simply be a case of deciding what really needs to be an issue and what isn't all that important in the greater scheme of things.

The ARs insistence at avoiding conflict and confrontation can sometimes make them a target for being the "soft touch" in the family. In many cases, ARs would simply "rather switch than fight." They do strive to keep everyone happy, and that can mean giving in on issues that may have been firmly enforced by the more sequential parent. Although ARs will usually stand firmly for the nonnegotiable issues of physical safety and moral and ethical values, almost everything else is really dependent on the day and the mood of the AR. Unfortunately, this may send mixed messages, especially to a more sequential child. The child may get in trouble for doing something one day and the next day it goes by completely unnoticed.

AR parents married to more sequential spouses often find themselves in conflict over issues of disciplining the children. ARs may feel they need to bend over backwards to soften the methods of the sequential parent. And the sequential spouse may continually feel like "the bad guy," because he or she has to enforce a structure that the AR tends to avoid.

ARs are usually very conscientious parents, and they often feel badly that they are asking their children to be organized and keep rooms clean, when the AR parents themselves are hard-pressed to do the same. It is relatively easy to make ARs feel guilty. Early in their lives, children can pick up on this, and unfortunately can master the art of manipulating the AR parent. ARs are very sensitive to how others feel, and it is both an asset and a liability to care so much about what others think.

THE ABSTRACT RANDOM CHILD

One mother good-naturedly complained that when her Abstract Random daughter got a teacher she liked, it turned out to be quite expensive. "At least twice a week, my daughter would tell me we needed to buy or make something nice for Mrs. Hughes because she'd had a rough day." After a year of gifts and thank-you notes, Mom had a new appreciation for her daughter's thoughtfulness and sensitivity. "However, next year, we're hoping our daughter gets a teacher who's a little more even tempered!" the mother admitted.

The Dominant Abstract Random child, probably more than any of the other learning styles, cares about pleasing people. For the AR child, all of life and learning is an intensely personal experience.

It is difficult for ARs to concentrate on learning something that doesn't appear to have any effect on their own life or the lives of people who matter to them. ARs may be motivated to get good grades simply because it means so much to their parents. They may frequently be accused of "not living up to your potential" because they rarely pursue knowledge purely for the love of learning.

In the nursing program at a local university, administrators discovered they were losing a lot of potentially good nursing candidates. Upon closer examination, they found that many of the dropouts were AR students. The ARs were drawn to the profession out of a sense of personal nurturing and devotion to the well-being of others. Unfortunately, no one really warned them about all the very *un*-AR classes that must be endured before they could successfully fulfill their dream. The professors decided to stay close to the AR students and coach them by reminding them why they wanted to become nurses in the first place—to save lives and make a difference. Somehow it made the classes in physics, chemistry, and anatomy personal challenges that must be met to achieve the ultimate goal. Almost everyone discovered that the AR can ace the most difficult class as long as there is a personal, passionate commitment to the outcome.

The AR child may have a difficult time in a classroom where other children are not happy or where they feel the teacher does not take a personal interest in or liking to them. It's almost like the AR has invisible antenna up at all times, scanning the atmosphere for trouble spots. If there is conflict or strife between personalities, it is almost impossible for the AR to concentrate on learning.

It is almost always the AR child who will come up to the teacher and say something like, "Susie's dog got run over this morning, and she's crying. Could we go into the other room so I can talk to her?" The CS or AS children may *also* point out Susie's distress, but usually they will say something like, "Susie's crying. Do you think you could get someone to go talk to her?" It doesn't take long for the other children to realize that it is the AR who can most naturally listen to and comfort those in need.

WHAT ABOUT STRESS?

When it comes to what causes and relieves stress, the dominant AR parent and child have a lot in common.

The Dominant Abstract Random usually thrives with

frequent, honest praise
reassurance of love and worth
opportunities to work together
opportunities to use creativity and imagination
acceptance of personal feelings and emotions

The Dominant Abstract Random is often stressed by

having to justify feelings
competing individually
not feeling liked or appreciated
pressure by loved ones to be more sequential

You can frequently lessen the stress by

allowing the AR to work together with someone else
noticing the good things without pointing out the bad
daily reassurance of love and value to the family and the world
just listening without offering unsolicited advice

ABSTRACT RANDOM

What People with Other Styles Admire Most

spontaneity

concern for others

sociability

adaptability

ability to understand
how others feel

Negative Perceptions by People with Other Styles

unpredictable

don't take a hard stand

overly sensitive to criticism

not aware of time limitations

smooth over problems rather than solve them

Ten Commandments for Getting Along with ARs

Thou shalt:

give me the opportunity to help others

give me feedback (positive/negative)—where do I stand?

not be so serious

not nit-pick

remember, I will get things done—even if it's not your way

not put me in the middle of a conflict

allow me to be spontaneous

show appreciation

not mistake a happy exterior for lack of intelligence

know that not all is written in stone

In a Nutshell

When it comes to being in touch with others, sensing what needs to be done, and getting along with difficult people, there don't seem to be any better candidates for sainthood than ARs. As one person put it, "When they gave out love and kindness, you ARs got double-dipped!" Other styles can sometimes sell the ARs short by not appreciating the spontaneity and flexibility that comes as part of the package. If we want to learn to get along with other people, each of us must daily use our AR skills.

Chapter Six

The Dominant
Concrete Random (CR)
Learning Style

The Concrete Sequential mom had just taken a big drink of juice when she made a horrible face and spit it out. "Ack! This tastes *awful*!" she said.

Her Concrete Random son reached for the glass. "Let me try it," he offered.

She looked at him as if he had lost his mind. "Don't you trust me?" she asked. "Why would you *want* to taste something I just told you was awful?"

It wasn't that her CR son didn't *trust* her—he just needed to *experience* facts in order to actually believe them.

THE DOMINANT CONCRETE RANDOM ADULT

The Dominant Concrete Random person is probably the least likely to take your word about anything. These people have a compelling need to experience as much for themselves as they possibly can. CRs, more than any other style, strive *not* to be ordinary. If you say that something is so for everyone, CRs will tell you that they are *not* everyone, so what is true for others,

61

is not necessarily true for them.

Because the CR lives in the "real world," usually anything that can't be experienced firsthand cannot be fully trusted. CRs are notorious risk takers. They believe you cannot break away from the ordinary unless you are willing to go out on a limb.

CRs are intuitive, quick-thinking, curious, and resourceful. The concrete part of their nature makes them very "hands-on," but their random ordering process causes them to be somewhat unpredictable. The CRs often fight structure and routine, preferring to keep all their options open. Life usually goes by at a breathless pace with CRs because they are constantly looking for new challenges and untried doors. If something becomes routine or boring, CRs simply drop it and go on to the next, more exciting prospect.

It's not unusual for CRs to have several careers in a lifetime, sometimes even two careers at once. It is not necessarily a lack of focus as much as a desire for variety, a sense of being able to conquer the unknown. The resourceful CR nature keenly grasps the obvious and can quickly turn it into something unexpected.

As I was driving home the other evening, I heard my two-and-a-half-year-old twin sons arguing in the back seat. Michael (CR extraordinaire) was hitting his AR brother, Robert. Although I suspected what was going on, I decided to give him the benefit of the doubt.

"Michael," I said sternly, "I'm pulling over and turning on the light. If you are hitting your brother, you are in big trouble." I stopped the car, switched on the light, and turned around to see Michael's hand resting on his brother's arm. With lightning-fast reflexes, Mike grinned at me and said, "*Tickle, tickle, tickle!*"

It was a perfect example of the CRs natural gift for getting in *and* out of trouble quickly. Because they can think so well on their feet, it is rare that you can catch them violating a given rule, even if they get off on a technicality.

CRs, for the most part, consider most rules to be simply guidelines. In their thinking, rules are for people who don't know how to do the right thing in the first place.

I am, admittedly, a strong CR. One year it was almost Christmas, and my AR sister Sandee, one of her small children, and I were Christmas shopping in a department store. When we got to the escalator with the stroller, Sandee noticed a sign that said, "No strollers allowed on the escalator." While she was reading the sign, I was busy loading the stroller onto the moving stairway.

Sandee was horrified. "The sign says no strollers on the escalator!" she cried.

I looked at her. "Oh, are the *stroller police* going to get us?" I asked sarcastically. "Sandee, this sign is for people who don't know how to safely put a stroller on an escalator. Since I *do* know how, it doesn't apply to me."

She refused to follow me upstairs for several minutes, not wanting anyone in the store to realize she was with someone who so blatantly disregarded a *rule*. For me, it was simply a *guideline*.

It is difficult for the CR to accept limits and restrictions, especially if the rules seem arbitrary or dictatorial. Most CRs believe in being law-abiding citizens and are especially conscious of setting a good example for their children. CRs have the most trouble with rules and regulations that do not seem to have practical reasons for their existence.

"Rank has its privileges" is *not* a CR motto, and "Just because I said so" is almost never accepted without challenge. The CR will not be deterred by the word *impossible* if he or she has determined the goal is a worthy one. At the other extreme, even the most accessible goal may be ignored by a CR who has decided achieving it is just not worth the trouble.

One young CR woman came up after a recent seminar and said, "I just have to tell you my own CR story!" She said that when she enrolled in a college chemistry class, she was surprised to hear the professor make a rather brash statement at the beginning of the first session. He told the students that since no one could possibly get an A on any test without doing the homework, the homework would count as 50 percent of the total semester grade.

This CR woman immediately bristled. *What did he mean it wasn't possible to get an A without doing the homework?* "Right then and there," she told me, "I decided I wasn't going to do a drop of homework. And I *did* get a A on every test."

I smiled at her and said, "But you got a C in the class, didn't you?"

She grinned. "Yep, but it was the best C I ever got!"

CRs sometimes frustrate people of more sequential styles because they don't go by the book, and they constantly seek to change the system or try something new. It is these very bents, however, that keep everyone growing and challenged to consider new and uncharted possibilities.

THE DOMINANT CONCRETE RANDOM PARENT

One evening, a young CR father read his four-year-old son, also a Concrete Random, a bedtime story and tucked him in. As the father left the room, the boy said, "Dad, leave the hall light on."

Dad replied, "No, son, we're not going to leave the hall light on."

"Yes, I want the hall light on."

"No, no hall light."

"Yes!"

"No!"

"Yes!"

"No!" And the hall light went off.

The boy started to cry. The parents decided he could jolly well cry himself to sleep. But two hours later, *everybody* was sick of it. The boy was tired of crying, but he wasn't going to give in. The parents were tired of listening to him, but it had been decided that the hall light was *not* going to go on.

Finally the father walked back down the hall, looked into the room, and discovered his son had uncovered one of his feet from the blanket. The teary-eyed little boy said, "Dad, if you'll cover my foot, I'll go to sleep."

So his dad covered his foot and the boy went to sleep. You see, the war was no longer worth winning—but for both CR parent and CR child, unconditional surrender was out of the question.

The father needed to maintain his authority as a parent, but his compromise allowed his CR son a graceful way to surrender the battle.

CR parents often find themselves frustrated by children who do not do what they are told. Now, mind you, CR parents would be the *last* to do something just because you said so. But once CRs have decided how something should be, they tend to issue ultimatums or orders that they themselves probably wouldn't obey.

CRs are passionate about their convictions. CR parents want the best for their children, but they can sometimes find themselves insisting that their children accept the CR way whether the children like it or not.

CRs often make fun and exciting playmates for their children, actively participating in almost everything and encouraging their children to play whatever game it is for all they're worth. Life for CRs is an adventure, and they will be the first to conquer uncharted territories and slay scary dragons.

Because CR parents understand the CR nature of their children, you would think they would get along well. Although they sometimes do, being alike is not always a benefit. Since the CR parent doesn't want to back down anymore than the CR child does, it often makes for an unflinching standoff between parent and child.

THE DOMINANT CONCRETE RANDOM CHILD

A kindergarten teacher gave her class a creative art assignment. "I want you to draw a picture of someone you really admire," she said. As many good teachers do, she had drawn a picture of someone *she* most admired, so the children could see an example. After most of the children were finished, the teacher found that almost everyone had copied her drawing. One little boy— a CR—was still working on his paper. When the teacher asked who he was drawing, he proudly replied, "This is a picture of God."

The teacher smiled a bit uncertainly and said, "But no one knows what God looks like."

The CR boy just beamed. "They will when I get through!"

The Dominant Concrete Random child is usually full of energy, curiosity, and new ideas. Boredom is the CRs greatest enemy, and school is often viewed as a prison sentence to be served. Formal education must be endured until one can escape into the real world and learn what *really* counts.

Although strong will comes in *all* styles, I have never, in over a decade of teaching learning styles, talked to any dominant CR child or adult who did not admit to being strong-willed. This does not mean CRs are openly rebellious or defiant, only very determined to stay in control of their own lives. CRs do not automatically reject rules and regulations, but they *do* expect to have at least some input into how the rules are made and enforced.

CRs have a nature that resists ultimatums. If you say "do this or *else*," CRs will most likely do "else." They may do it quietly, without fuss, but CRs know there is nothing they really *have* to do except die. Which, by the way, they are willing to do if necessary. Most other styles are not willing to perish over the small things, but CRs are.

When I was younger, my mother and I had a recurring conflict about my messy bedroom. As long as I could find the bed, it was clean enough for me. However, my mother's definition of clean meant I would have to do a lot more than just be able to find the bed. It meant work.

My room was the source of many arguments between us. One day I decided, out of the blue, that I wanted to do something really nice and unexpected for my mother. I determined to clean my bedroom just the way she had always wanted me to do it. Wouldn't that be a wonderful surprise? On the way to my room, my mother intercepted me. It had been a bad day. She was up to her neck in dirty rooms.

Pointing her finger at me, she said, "Cynthia Kay Ulrich, get in your room *right now*. You are not coming out of there until that room is clean."

What I was inspired to do just moments before had suddenly become an ultimatum. I saw it as an edict designed to take all control away from me. I decided there was nothing my mother could do that would compel me to clean my room.

I took the punishment: I got spanked. I got grounded. I went without dinner. Nothing worked. My mother probably could have, at that point, struck a match and set the room on fire and I'd have chosen to perish in the flames.

I had not set out to deliberately disobey my mother. It was only when I felt I had no control that I refused to cooperate. The ultimatum had been issued, and I felt I had no choice but to prove I did not *have* to obey.

The CRs concrete abilities make them masters at separating the letter from the spirit of the law. It is a great resource for accomplishing what the CR wants to do without *technically* having done anything against the rules. "You said don't jump off *this* chair."

Carol, one of the teachers attending one of my classes about teaching strong-willed children, recalled an incident in her childhood that remains a vivid example of her strong-willed, CR nature. She was in elementary school, and the teacher was passing around a pussy willow for the children to look at closely. The teacher told the class that everyone should feel free to touch and play with the pussy willow, but *whatever* they did, they were *not* to put the pussy willow in their ear. Carol was the last one to get the pussy willow. While waiting for her turn to hold it, she almost drove herself crazy wondering *why* the teacher said not to put it in her ear. Why not? What would happen?

When the pussy willow finally got to her, Carol scrunched down in her seat, hid her face, and stuck it not in her ear, but in her nose. It went in easy, but it got stuck coming out, and she ended up having to stand in the corner for quite a while for her little experiment. To this day, she says she feels angry with that teacher. After all, she did *not* put the pussy willow in her *ear*, so she had *not* disobeyed!

Although CR children can easily exasperate their parents, the fact is that CRs expect parents to be in authority. CRs expect boundaries and actually welcome the security of knowing the limits. The greatest challenge comes in how parents communicate that authority, and how much input the CR has into the rules and the consequences.

Several years ago, I was sitting in a family restaurant with my husband when I overheard a heated conversation at the next table. I glanced over and saw a young mom and dad and a small boy about eight years old. The dad slammed his fork down and pointed his finger at his son. "You do this to me every time," he said. "I let you order on your own from the child's menu, and then you don't eat what you order. Well, I'll tell you what, young man, from now on *I'll* do the ordering and *you'll* do the eating."

The boy did not acknowledge that he had heard the new rule at all. His father leaned closer to him. "And we're not leaving here until you've eaten what you ordered today."

I sneaked a look at that young boy's face. Without uttering a word, his expression said, "Bring on the rent receipt book; I guess we live here now." The ultimatum had been given, and the boy obviously had no intention of complying. The father's back was toward me, and I could see the flush begin to creep up his neck. The veins began to bulge, and he was almost shaking with his anger. The mom seemed upset at the turn of events. I could tell she had played this scene many times before. Attempting to smooth the waters, she reached out to her son. "Maybe if you eat something from *my* plate," she began. *"Don't you help him!"* roared the father. *"He's going to do this on my terms!"*

A few minutes later, I watched this family leave the restaurant. The father stormed out, practically on the verge of a cardiac arrest. The mother was in tears, and the child, wearing an indifferent expression, had left behind an uneaten dinner.

I understood the situation better than most. As a mother, I certainly can empathize with those parents. But as a lifelong strong-willed child, I can tell you that in most cases the approach they used does not work.

If I had been that strong-willed child, do you know what would have worked with me? If my dad had said, "Are you going to eat that?" and I had replied, "No," my dad's response would then have been to call the waitress and ask for a doggie bag. He would have turned to me and said, "Fine. You don't have to eat it now, but it *will* be the next thing you eat. You see, the rule is you eat what you order. That's the rule." If my dad let me have some control in deciding under what *terms* I would eat it, he would usually find me complying with the rule. It really is more an issue of control than of authority.

WHAT ABOUT STRESS?

When it comes to recognizing and dealing with stress, the dominant CR parent and child have a lot in common.

The Dominant Concrete Random usually thrives with

inspiration
independence
compelling reasons
freedom to choose options
guidelines instead of rules
opportunities for creative alternatives

The Dominant Concrete Random is often stressed by

excessive restrictions and limitations
forced schedules or routines
not being appreciated as a unique individual
not being given credit for knowing the right thing to do

You can frequently lessen the stress by

lightening up without letting up
backing off, not forcing the issue
helping the CR figure out what will inspire him
encouraging lots of ways to reach the same goal
conveying love and acceptance no matter what

CONCRETE RANDOM

What People with Other Styles Admire Most About the CR

sense of humor

multidimensional personality

creativity

intuition

independence

Negative Perceptions By People with Other Styles

uncompromising

not a team player

too many whys

stubborn

impulsive

Ten Commandments for Getting Along with a CR

Thou Shalt:

keep me involved (we need responsibility and input)

have a sense of humor

tell me "what" not "how"

be open to change

point me in the right direction, then let me go

be flexible

tell me what I did right, not what I did wrong

why do we need ten?

don't be threatened by enthusiasm

know your limits—then push them

Now that you have some understanding of learning styles and have hopefully identified your own, take a piece of paper and draw a picture that illustrates some of the characteristics of your child's or your own learning style. To get you started, here is a picture that represents the characteristics of an Abstract Random learning style. *We are only using the AR style as an example.* If you are a different learning style, your picture will look very different.

Save your picture. We will be adding more learning style elements to it as we go along.

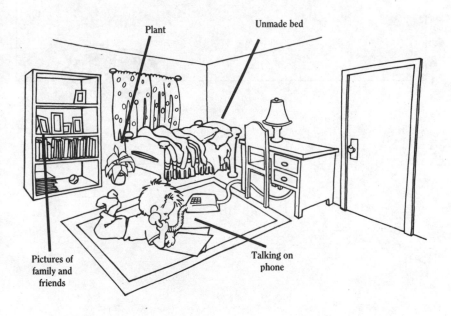

In a Nutshell

I frequently tell parents of strong-willed, CR children that those kids are going to change the world. It's not likely the world is going to change *them*! Once you begin to understand CR strengths, you will be amazed at how much CRs contribute to keeping the world moving and growing and changing. Instead of fighting to force CRs to conform, perhaps we should take a little more notice of how many of their ideas have real merit. The CR in all of us may just save us from ourselves!

Chapter Seven

How Do We Concentrate?

Now that you have a basic grasp of Gregorc's description of how our minds work, let me add another layer to the overall picture. We all have certain preferences for our most productive learning environments. Such things as the way a room is lighted or heated, if the chairs are comfortable or not, if we are hungry or not, can all influence our ability to concentrate.

Identifying these environmental preferences will add an important dimension to our understanding of learning styles.

Several years ago, I tuned into an afternoon talk show touting an educational consultant. He had just written a book designed to help parents get their reluctant children to do homework. The producer had invited several sets of frustrated mothers and their children. The host let the author and the mothers interact with each other candidly.

Although each mother's story was different, the "homework expert" repeated the same solution for everyone: "Make the task of doing homework an absolutely relentless pursuit. Outline to your child what is expected, and don't give up until he or she has made this a habit."

One mother had her 12-year-old son by the shoulders. "But my son gets distracted by *everything!*" she exclaimed. The homework expert shook his head. "Then you aren't making this whole procedure important enough in your family routine," he admonished. The already frustrated mother made an exasperated gesture and guided her son off the stage.

Another harried mother spoke up. "I have tried *everything* to get my daughter to do her homework short of threatening to *kill* her. *Nothing* works." The expert smiled indulgently and insisted, "You just have to make it important enough."

One by one I watched the mothers leave in despair, certain that not only was their child not doing homework, but that it was somehow their *fault* for not being firm enough or dedicated enough to finding a solution.

Getting children to do homework illustrates how difficult it can be for them to concentrate and focus on learning. Although many factors have been blamed for this lack of attention, I believe that perhaps the most logical, reasonable causes have been largely overlooked.

As parents, it is quite natural for us to insist that our children study and approach learning tasks in the ways that make sense to *us*. After all, we are living proof of what does and does not work. Right?

But think about it. How many of you who are reading this book married someone exactly like you? It is rare. (Isn't it interesting how we are drawn to those so different from us for their "refreshing perspective," and then find ourselves so annoyed by the contrasts between our styles on a day-to-day basis?) Now if you and your spouse are so dramatically different in your approaches to life, just think of the myriad of combinations your children will exhibit!

But wait! All is not lost! We can learn to use our children's choices of *environmental preferences* to help them concentrate and learn. Let's look at some different study environments and see which are best when a person really needs to concentrate and learn effectively.

Among the leading researchers in this field is the husband and wife team of Kenneth and Rita Dunn.[1] The Dunns have spent years studying the effects of environment on an individual and the individual's inborn learning style as it relates to concentration and remembering information. (See the bibliography for more on this topic.) Using the Dunn's research, let me highlight a few important factors every parent should consider while trying to find the most effective way to help their children concentrate.

WHERE SHOULD YOUR CHILDREN STUDY?

The traditional idea of giving our children a suitable place to study has been around for generations. The standard approach is to insist upon a consistent time each evening, provide a clean, quiet, well-lit room with a desk and chair, and make sure the room and the child are free of distractions. For many children, as well as adults, this is a very effective way to concentrate. For some of us, however, it is tantamount to being imprisoned without possibility of parole.

I have always favored working on the floor, both as a student and as an adult. Even if I'm dressed in a business suit, I close my office door and spread everything out on the floor before commencing my work. At home, my husband will often find me hunched over books and papers on the floor, lost in thought. He is concerned.

"The light is terrible in here!" he exclaims. "And you're going to ruin your back sitting on the floor like that. Here, here! We have a perfectly clean and wonderful rolltop desk." He sweeps up my papers and neatly places them on the desk, helps me into the chair, turns on the high-intensity lamp, and pats my shoulder.

"Now, isn't that better?" he asks.

I nod and wait until he is down the hall and out of sight. Then, I gather all my papers and go back down on the floor. You see, I could sit at the rolltop desk for as long as he really needed me to sit there. But that's all I'd be doing—sitting at the rolltop desk. I could sit there for an hour, and when he came back, I wouldn't have done anything. "What's the matter?" he'd ask. "You've had ideal conditions: an hour of uninterrupted time and a clean, well-lit place to work. Why haven't you *done* anything?" It does not occur to him that anyone in their right mind could actually work better on the floor than on the desk, or concentrate better in 10-minute spurts with music or noise in the background than in a silent 60-minute block of time.

Sitting on the couch or curling up on the floor is the only way some people can be comfortable enough to really concentrate. Because of our individual preferences, it's important to remember that *our* way won't always work for everybody in our family. Instead of insisting on a particular place for your child to study, try watching what position your child uses most often when engrossed in a book or other favorite task, and let him use the same position for studying.

How Quiet Should It Be?

Some parents have a hard time imagining that a person could actually *need* noise to keep from being distracted. I, for one, am greatly distracted by solitude and silence. My husband, on the other hand, is *dependent* upon those two elements for any constructive task. We have yet to see what kind of study environment our sons will need. Because they are not alike, except in the way they look, they will probably each have a very different environmental work preference.

Often parents will express surprise that their children seem to get the most homework done while sitting in the middle of the living room with the television on and other family members coming and going. Many students tell me they do their best work while lying comfortably on a bed. Others claim they have to be sitting in hard chairs in order to stay alert.

What About Light?

At some point in our lives, most of us have heard our moms tell us, "Turn on the light or you'll ruin your eyes!" The truth is, we all seem to have different levels of tolerance for bright or dim light. In most families, there is at least one person who goes around turning *off* lights behind the person who is turning *on* every light in the house. Although public schools insist upon using bright overhead florescent lights, some students may *lose* concentration because they need a softer light. Experiment with different levels of light in order to find out what is most comfortable and produces the best learning environment for your child. The key is to use enough light to see without having to strain your eyes. Remember, the chances are very good that *your* preferences will be different from those of your children!

Should You Turn up the Heat?

If you walk into almost any classroom around the country, you will usually find some students sitting comfortably in lightweight, short-sleeved shirts while others are shivering in their sweaters or jackets.

When it comes to an ideal room temperature, there are physical differences between individuals. If the temperature is too hot or too cold, many students will be unable to concentrate. While some adapt easily to varying temperatures, others need the room to be comfortable before they can pay attention to anything else.

One of my favorite anecdotes was related during a workshop by Rita Dunn, the researcher I mentioned earlier in this chapter. As she was working with young students who were studying English as a second language, she was trying to test their knowledge of basic words. "What is a 'sweater'?" she asked the children. One small boy near the front immediately raised his hand and answered matter-of-factly: "It's what your mother makes you wear when she's cold."

Should Students Be Allowed to Eat While Studying?

It has been a long-standing rule in traditional classrooms that no food or drink is allowed. For some children, this is not a problem, since eating or drinking might distract them from listening and concentrating. For others, however, eating or drinking may actually be necessary to keep their minds focused on what they are doing. If you need to have a cup of coffee or can of soda handy while working, you probably understand why many students are distracted when they must listen to a teacher or work on an assignment when they are hungry or thirsty.

If you see a student chewing on a pencil or gnawing on the end of a ruler, it could be that he or she is desperately trying not to think about the hunger pangs that are threatening to overshadow any academic thoughts. Although it's not always practical to have food and drink in a classroom, often just a piece of hard candy or chewing gum is enough to help a hungry student concentrate on what's being taught instead of thinking about the lunch break.

LISTENING TO THE INTERNAL TIME CLOCK

Since I have always been a morning person, I was surprised to find out that there are those who are actually *annoyed* by people who appear too alert or cheerful before 10 A.M. On the other hand, I'm ready to call it a day before the 11 o'clock news, while the night people are just getting their greatest spurt of energy. Although we can discipline ourselves to cope at just about any time of day, most of us have certain hours when we are naturally more energetic.

If you have one child who is most alert in the morning and another child who is the proverbial night owl, it's unrealistic to expect them both to do their best job on homework at the same time of day. It also stands to reason that when a student needs to take a difficult or boring class, he will succeed better if that class is scheduled during his most alert time of day. If that is impossible, he may at least be able to do his homework during his peak performance hours. If he can, his concentration will be greatly improved.

Recently, I met with several classes of high school students to discuss study skills. I set up the following scenario:

> Suppose you are wavering between an A and a B for a semester grade in history. The upcoming final exam will determine your semester grade. If you get an A on the final, you will get an A for the semester. If you get anything lower than an A on the final, your semester grade will be a B.
>
> Your parents are quite anxious that you get the highest possible grade for the semester. They're so eager, that they've promised you a car in exchange for your outstanding performance on the final. Take the large sheet of paper and draw a picture of where you will study for this all-important test. Draw in as much detail as possible: location, lighting, refreshments, etc., in your ideal study spot.

When the students finished, they initialed their drawings and posted them. Several students were given the opportunity to explain their ideal study situations. Throughout the sharing, students who were not sharing kept exclaiming, "You study in your bedroom? No way! I'd fall asleep if I tried that!" or "I have to have daylight or I just can't concentrate," or "I could never study *outside*!" When the discussion was over, I asked them an important question:

"So, what *is* the right study situation?" The answer was simple and unanimous. "It's the one that works best for *you*."

A RADICAL EXPERIMENT FOR GETTING YOUR CHILD TO DO HOMEWORK

Many parents say that their children have some pretty ridiculous claims about where and when they *like* to do homework. These parents wonder how anyone can work late at night on the couch with a can of pop and the radio on. If getting your child to do homework is becoming an almost impossible chore, here is an approach that may at first seem a bit radical. But keep an open mind!

Strike a deal with your reluctant student. For two weeks, agree to let the student study at home any *time*, in any *place*, with any *thing* he or she says is needed (within the laws of the land and the rules of the household, of course). If, at the end of that two weeks, he turns in his homework and his grades are improving, you will accept that your child really *does* know how to study best. If, however, homework is still *not* being turned in and grades are *not* improving, the student must agree to abide by *your* study methods.

For best results, contact your child's teacher before the two-week period begins. Discuss what you're proposing, and ask the teacher to help you judge whether or not your child's work improves or goes downhill during the trial period.

I find that although students may begin by trying some pretty outrageous methods during the first two or three days, they also realize they must prove that their ways *work*. In the end, many will actually move closer to the methods their parents had in mind in the first place. Interestingly enough, parents find *they* have been able to effectively compromise in ways that may never have occurred to them.

One frustrated mother claimed her daughter was simply trying to use her learning style as an excuse to watch a favorite television show. "My daughter says she can only do her hardest homework during this half-hour television show." I suggested she call her daughter's bluff. If it was a television show approved by her parents, let her do her homework during the show. At the end of the show, however, collect the homework. After all, the daughter must prove her claim is true. Accountability must stay intact!

A Note: It's important to remember that not all of these categories of environmental preferences are equally important to all people. Certain environmental factors may matter a great deal to some. Other factors may just be a bonus. For example, I concentrate better when I can eat or drink something while I am working, but I *can* work without it. I can't work at *all* if I'm cold. Try to identify the elements that are absolutely essential to your child's ability to concentrate successfully. Then, work at achieving as many environmental preferences as possible, as often as possible.

Remember, too, that children should not be able to use their learning styles as an excuse to avoid doing something that doesn't come naturally or sound fun. If you define the specific outcomes you want your children to accomplish, you can then help them achieve those outcomes in a way that makes the most sense to *their* natural learning styles. The chances for their success will be much greater. In circumstances where you cannot accommodate your children's natural learning styles, you can help them understand and cope with the demands of doing whatever they must by recognizing, and then talking with them, about *why* they may find the task frustrating. You can show them how to identify and use their natural strengths to do those things that don't come easily for them.

PUTTING IT INTO ACTION

The following suggestions can help you identify some of your child's natural environmental preferences. As you work through these suggestions, you may discover some of your *own* learning style strengths. Sharing *your* preferences with your child can help both of you understand and appreciate your similarities and differences.

- Give your child a large piece of paper and some markers or crayons. Ask your child to draw a picture of the ideal study place. Ask for as many specific details as possible, and let your child have the opportunity to explain the drawing to you.
- If your child is finding it difficult to identify his preferences, it may help to set up situations that contrast the differences. For example, have

your child try doing a portion of homework in a brightly-lit room and another portion in an area where the lights are at a lower level. Ask him which lighting made it easier to concentrate. (Be prepared for the answer "It doesn't matter." Remember, sometimes it really doesn't.)

- Challenge your child to design, create, or describe the ideal study spot at home. Then, as much as is possible, try to make it become a reality.

Find the drawing you made when you finished the last chapter. Now add some elements that show your most important environmental preferences. Do you need a lot of light? Do you like the room to be warm?

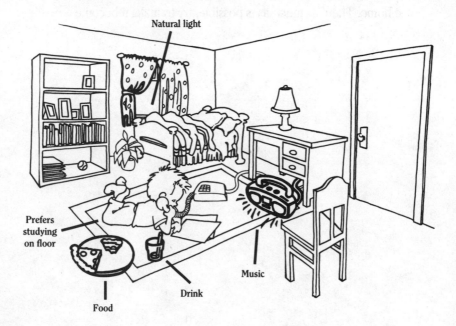

Natural light

Prefers studying on floor

Food

Drink

Music

In a Nutshell

Not everyone benefits from the same circumstances and surroundings when it is necessary to concentrate and work. The bottom line is this: Do you know what works for you? Do you know what works for each of your children? Even if you have to change your idea of what "good studying" looks like, you may discover that more homework gets done in an environment that fits individual learning style. You may even find out that some of us *need* chaos to accomplish order!

Chapter Eight

How Do We Remember?

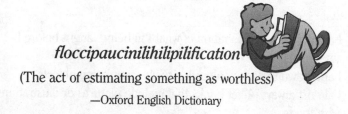

floccipaucinilihilipilification

(The act of estimating something as worthless)

—Oxford English Dictionary

How long would it take you to learn how to spell this word? How would you remember it? Would it be important for you to hear the word pronounced before you learned to spell it?

We use a variety of our five senses when processing and memorizing facts and figures. This is called *sensory perception*. In other words, when we *perceive,* or take in information, we are using one or more of our senses to understand and remember what we perceived.

Here is yet another dimension that can add to our overall understanding of natural learning style strengths and preferences. While Gregorc's model gave us insight into how our minds work and the Dunns' model showed us the diversity of environmental preferences, this model will help us learn several ways of remembering information.

Take this test to determine if you and your children are auditory, visual, or kinesthetic learners.

MODALITY CHECKLIST

Place a check mark by all the statements that strongly describe what you prefer.

Auditory

__I need to hear myself say it in order to remember it.

__I often need to talk through a problem aloud in order to solve it.

__I memorize best by repeating the information aloud or to myself over and over.

__I remember best when the information fits into a rhythmic or musical pattern.

__I would rather listen to a recording of a book than sit and read it.

Visual

__I need to see an illustration of what I'm being taught before I understand it.

__I am drawn to flashy, colorful, visually stimulating objects.

__I almost always prefer books that include pictures or illustrations with the text.

__I look like I'm "daydreaming," when I'm trying to get a mental picture of what's being said.

__I usually remember better when I can actually see the person who's talking.

Kinesthetic

__I have difficulty sitting still for more than a few minutes at a time.

__I usually learn best by physically participating in a task.

__I almost always have some part of my body in motion.

__I prefer to read books or hear stories that are full of action.

Learning styles researchers Walter Barbe and Raymond Swassing[1] present three modes of sensory perception (ways of remembering) that we all use in varying degrees. These are referred to as *modalities*. The most easily recognized modalities are: auditory, visual, and kinesthetic. Let's take a closer look at each of these.

Auditory — Learning by listening to verbal instructions; remembering by forming the sounds of words.

If you are a strong auditory learner, this does *not* necessarily mean you only need to hear something once to remember it. It *does* mean that in most circumstances you need to hear *yourself* say it in order to effectively commit it to memory. If your auditory mode is particularly strong, you may find yourself reading aloud instead of silently, talking to yourself, or repeating instructions to make sure you understand them.

If you have a more auditory child, you may find that putting facts or dates into a song, a rap, or a rhythm of some kind helps them memorize. Listening to how a word *sounds* may be a very important part of learning what the word *means*.

During my years as a police officer, one of my specialties was finding and arresting drunk drivers. A crucial part of determining whether or not a driver was too intoxicated to be behind the wheel was the "field sobriety test." After I put the suspected drunk driver through a variety of balance tests, I always asked the same question at the end. "Could you please say the alphabet for me?"

You see, unless you are a rare case or a hardened alcoholic, you usually can't say the alphabet at a normal conversational rate if you're under the influence of alcohol. If drunk driving weren't so serious, it would have been almost amusing to hear the various versions of the standard alphabet these inebriated individuals recited. Interestingly enough, it seems as though no matter how drunk a person is, he can almost always *sing* the alphabet song. I had more than one person in a business suit standing by the side of the road singing his ABCs just so he could remember how the alphabet started!

It might be wise to insert a word of caution here. Often a strongly auditory parent insists that the not-so-auditory child drills or reviews aloud. If the auditory mode is not particularly strong in the child, he may have to struggle to memorize using this method. In other words, at the end of those precious minutes carved out of a busy evening, you may have a child who knows *less* than when the review began! The frustrated parent believes that the child is simply not paying attention or not trying hard enough to remember. And the child may not even be able to explain *why* he can't remember.

Visual   Learning by seeing and watching; using strong visual associations.

If the *visual* way of learning is particularly strong for you, you may often try to picture in your mind what you are learning. You may even be accused of daydreaming or being lost in thought. The more visual learner usually learns best by associating pictures with the words or concepts being used. When reading or remembering, the visual learner may constantly be imagining what things *look* like and may sometimes be picturing something *very* different than the actual facts!

Because I am a strong visual learner, I began to keep a written record of the names of places that evoked strong mental pictures, even though I realized the images in my mind were probably not entirely accurate. For example, I get a warm, full feeling when I see the street sign in Nampa, Idaho, that tells me I'm walking down *Chicken Dinner Road*. It is not, however, a very positive image that pops into my mind when I read the name of one of the long-standing, used-car lots in Boise: *Fairly Reliable Bob's*. But by far my most vivid visual conjecture is when I drive south of downtown Seattle past a large green building sporting a big sign identifying it as the *Buffalo Sanitary Wipers Company*. Wow! Talk about mental images!

If you have a child who tends to learn more visually, you may find it helpful to encourage the use of brightly colored folders for categorizing papers or eye-catching notebooks for organizing assignments. When reviewing for a test, your visual child may find it most effective to use brightly-colored flashcards. This can help your child concentrate on a visual image for each fact or concept that must be memorized. Even if you're not much of an artist, it often helps the strong visual learner to draw a quick picture that can be associated with what needs to be remembered.

Kinesthetic
Learning by becoming physically involved and actually *doing* something with what's being learned.

If you have a child whose *kinesthetic* modality is strongest, you may find him in almost constant motion. All his life he has probably been accused of being "fidgety" or a "wiggle worm." The kinesthetic person hears things like "Sit still!" "Put your feet on the floor!" "No more trips to the drinking fountain!" Although most teachers and parents work hard to get children to be still, the strong kinesthetic child needs to put some sort of action to the learning or the learning doesn't stick! Even if the action is as simple as pacing or moving while reading or memorizing, the more kinesthetic learner will remember best what he learned while on the move.

Anne, a very kinesthetic friend of mine (now a physical education teacher!), admitted that her parents were pretty frustrated with her seemingly endless movements. Her mother would insist Anne stay in her bedroom in the basement until all her homework was done. Finally, this resourceful and restless learner devised a way to learn and still keep moving. She used the basement stairs. For spelling or vocabulary, each stair was a letter or word. For history, each was an important fact or date. For geography, each became a different location. Her mother was puzzled as to why Anne was constantly pounding up and down the stairs. All she knew was that Anne's homework was being done and her grades were improving!

Most strongly kinesthetic children are only able to concentrate on one thing for about 10 minutes at a time without taking some sort of break. Since physical activity is so important, if you are the parent of a kinesthetic child, you may want to suggest he put his homework on a clipboard and do it "on the run." Simply set a specific deadline for the homework to be finished, and let your active child burn up energy while learning! When your child must memorize important information, try associating some sort of bodily movement with what needs to be remembered.

IT REALLY WORKS!

I had been a high school English teacher for three years and was teaching a class called "Intermediate Composition." The class consisted of juniors and seniors who were not motivated enough for advanced composition and not unmotivated enough for the basic class. The administration had all but said that I should not be concerned about making much progress. I was to just do my best to get them through the class so they could graduate. One of my favorite classroom activities was vocabulary exercises. I was determined they would learn to speak and read on a more "educated" level. Each week the students would grudgingly take their vocabulary test, and each week the scores remained very poor.

Toward the end of the semester, I attended a learning conference where the keynote speaker was a learning styles expert. I sat spellbound throughout her presentation. Here was an educator and researcher who suddenly validated what I, as a teacher, had known for a long time: All students *could* learn, but we cannot expect them to learn in the same *way*. This speaker suggested practical methods for different *modality* approaches when trying to teach something that must be memorized.

Back in the classroom on Monday morning, I enthusiastically tried to communicate the information I had learned to my less-than-enthusiastic students. We were getting ready to take the semester test on 84 difficult vocabulary words. Because the weekly tests had resulted in such poor grades, none of the students expected to do much more than barely pass the semester test. I was so sold on this learning styles method that my students became intrigued in spite of themselves. I admitted the whole idea was new to me. I asked them if they would go along with me as an experiment and try studying the vocabulary words for the semester exam in a new way.

I explained to them the three different modalities: auditory, visual, and kinesthetic. I had each student fill out an informal checklist and then speculate on which modality or modalities were strongest for him or her. Then I told them my plan: For the next three days we would devote class time to studying the vocabulary words. To do that we would divide into study groups and each of the groups would use the method that made the most sense for that group's particular modality strength. A student could spend any amount of time in a group and could freely switch to another group.

These were the guidelines for the modality groups:

The *auditory group* drilled each other aloud. Back and forth, one student would say the word, and another would give the definition. There was constant noise in the group, as almost everyone was trying to verbalize the words and their meanings. Fortunately, we had access to an additional room where the auditory group could speak without disturbing the others.

The *visual group* carefully wrote flash cards for each vocabulary word, illustrating each card with an appropriate picture or design. For most of them, the very act of writing and illustrating the cards was enough to help them memorize the words, but they happily used the flash cards to quiz each other.

The *kinesthetic group* was a restless one! Since they preferred to stay in constant motion, I suggested they design body movements for each vocabulary word that would help them remember the definition. They eagerly accepted the challenge and sometimes literally wrestled over how their movements should define the vocabulary words.

The day of the final exam arrived. Normally on the day of a big test, I would hear at least two kinds of pleas from students as they entered: "Oh, please, can we have another day?" or "Quick! Give me the test before it all leaks out!"

That day the students sauntered in confidently, saying, "Bring on the test—I'm ready!" Twenty-nine heads bent to complete the test. I was amused as I watched the kinesthetic group of students take it. They were in constant motion, and at each word, they would pause, their bodies taking on a definite (and often mystifying) pose. Then they would mark an answer and go on.

Out of 29 "mediocre" students, 26 of them did not miss one single item on the test. Among the other three students, no one missed more than five. I had never seen my class so excited! Students who had never gotten an A in their academic life were heady with success. We all discussed why the methods worked and then celebrated with a pizza party.

Feeling somewhat euphoric, I shared my success in the faculty room with several of my fellow teachers. Their responses were like a bucket of cold water being thrown in my face. "The test was probably too easy." "You probably did the studying for them." "They probably cheated." "A fluke—it'll never happen again."

Feeling cheated out of my victory, I mulled over my options. How could I be sure my students really knew the information? Two weeks later, without warning, I gave these same students another test over the same words in a different test format. The grades were almost identical. The students were hurt that I would doubt their knowledge. "Miss Ulrich, we *know* those words!"

Mike was one of my seniors that year, and after graduating, he joined the Navy. For the next two years, each time Mike was home on leave he would show up at the door of my classroom after school. "Hey!" he'd say, "do you still have a copy of that vocabulary test?" I'd pull out the test, and he would quickly mark the answers and proudly present it for scoring. The result? Almost always 82 correct out of 84 (he had trouble with *imminent* vs. *eminent*). He'd grin at me and say, "See? I *told* you I know those words!"

Not all my learning style experiments had such dramatic results, but the learning curve increased *significantly* in most cases. Since my opportunities for varying the style of instruction I used were somewhat limited by administrative policies, I held my own parent/teacher meetings once a month. I helped interested parents develop some support strategies they could use at home for helping their children be more successful in school. Let me share a few of my favorites:

For more auditory learners:

- Offer to drill them verbally, or let them choose a classmate or friend who will drill with them.
- Help them put the information into a rhythmic pattern—perhaps create a poem, a song, or a rap.
- For reading assignments, let them read aloud, maybe even into a tape recorder, and then play it back for review.
- Minimize visual distractions in the study area.

For more visual learners:

- Give them bright colors and large spaces to draw or write.
- Encourage them to take notes or doodle while listening.
- Stress underlining or highlighting information in notes or books when possible so they can draw their own picture (no matter how bad they think it looks) to associate with facts, letters, or words.

For more kinesthetic learners:

- Encourage them to take frequent breaks while studying.
- Offer big spaces to draw and write.
- Provide them with stories to read that are filled with action.
- Instruct them to write notes or highlight information while listening.

There are three ways in which we take in and remember information. They are: auditory, visual, and kinesthetic. Add to your picture elements that illustrate how you take in information. You can be a CS, an AS, an AR, or a CR and can take in information in any of the three ways listed above. Now let's see what the AR in our example does. He is a strongly visual AR learner.

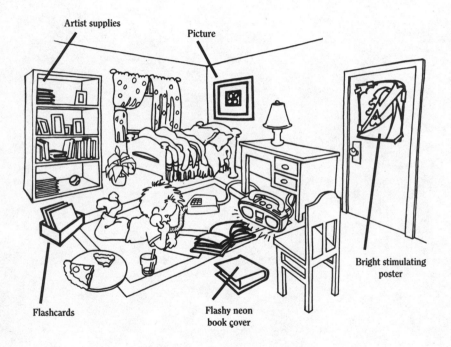

Artist supplies

Picture

Bright stimulating poster

Flashcards

Flashy neon book çover

In a Nutshell

Most people find they are strong in at least two of these modalities, and maybe even all three. No one is restricted to just one modality strength! If you aren't sure whether the auditory, visual, or kinesthetic methods would work best for your child, try out each approach until you find the one that fits. It may even vary from day to day. The important thing is to find the method of remembering and reviewing that works best for each individual!

Chapter Nine

How Do We Understand?

"Can you tell me where to find the library?"

"Sure! Just go down two blocks to the park with the statue in the middle, you know—where they tore the road up last year. Take a right until you get just past the fire station, then go about three more blocks until you see a great big white house with a green picket fence. The library is right across the street."

"I'm sorry, I'm a little confused. Can you tell me street names? Can you give me the address of the library?"

"Huh? Nope. Sorry—I only know how to get there!"

We have already looked at several ways to identify learning styles. The next layer of information can give you a solid grasp on the way you and your children deal with information from the very beginning. As we can see in the story above, when we learn, a fundamental difference occurs in the way each of us takes in and communicates the data. The way in which we take in information affects how we communicate it to others. The Witkin model of learning styles can help us recognize and appreciate this process.

This chapter is dedicated to helping you understand that learners of all ages can benefit by recognizing and using inborn learning strengths for tackling almost any task, assignment, or test. As we focus on the parent/student and teacher/student relationship, you may find unexpected reasons your child is experiencing success or frustration when it comes to learning.

During World War II, the United States Navy made a startling discovery about their fighter pilots. All of these pilots were exceptionally intelligent, incredibly talented, extremely motivated, rigidly screened, and thoroughly trained. However, when flying through a fog bank, some of these pilots would fly out of the mist upside down. This *concerned* the Navy! They could not afford to have pilots in the air who lost their whole sense of being upright when they lost their external field of vision.

The Navy called in a psychological researcher, Herman Witkin,[1] to conduct some tests on the pilots to determine which of them should be flying and which needed more instrument training before they got into any more cloud covers.

Witkin designed a special room for his experiments. He placed each pilot in a chair that tilted inside a room that also tilted. When the pilot was sure he was sitting straight up and down, he was to tell Witkin. Some of these pilots would claim they were sitting straight, and yet when Witkin checked, they and the room were actually tilted—sometimes as much as 30 degrees! They needed the room to be lined up with them in order to feel that they were sitting straight.

It's a lot like the sensation you get at Disneyland's "America the Beautiful" round theater. You're clutching the railing trying to keep from falling off the back of the fire truck you see on the screen. If the lights in the theater came on, you might feel a little silly! Nothing is actually moving. You are standing still and the only thing that's really changed is your external field of vision.

Other pilots tested by Witkin *always* knew when they were sitting straight up, no matter how tilted the room was. Evidently they were not affected as much by their external field of vision as the first set of pilots. This experiment began strictly as a test of physical perception. Almost by accident, Witkin and his associates began to notice some behaviors and traits that were consistent between these two types of pilots when they lost their external field of vision, and the way in which they approached learning tasks.

The pilots who always knew when they were sitting straight regardless of their surroundings tended to be more *field independent*, or *analytic*, when learning new information. They automatically broke down any information given them into component parts and then focused on details. The other pilots, those who needed their external field of vision in order to know when they were sitting straight, tended to approach information in a much more *field dependent*, or *global*, way. That is, they got the overall picture or "gist" of things, but they didn't worry about the details as much. Remember, both types of pilots were intelligent, talented, and motivated. The difference lay not in whether they *could* learn, but how they naturally learned *best*.

Because each person sees the world from his or her own frame of reference (global or analytic), it is possible that even when many people see the same event, they'll have several versions of what actually happened.

As a police officer, I helped investigate many automobile accidents. I would pull up to the scene, locate witnesses, and then begin the challenge of finding out what actually happened. The first witness might give me an accurate description of the cars involved—the year, the make, the model, the color. The next witness wouldn't have a clue about the kind of cars they were, but would launch into a detailed description of each driver. The third witness would look a little embarrassed at not noticing the cars and drivers, but couldn't wait to relate how the accident *happened*.

Did these people see the same accident? Yes, but these varying perspectives reflect the same learning differences the pilots experienced. The people who witnessed the accident were looking at the situation through their own "windows." The analytics were automatically recording details in their minds; the globals were naturally more concerned with the overall picture of what had happened.

As students, the way we approach learning and the effectiveness of our studying and taking tests is also greatly influenced by our natural tendency toward being more *global* or *analytic*. Naturally, no one person is purely one style or the other. But if we can identify some strengths and natural inclinations, we may discover more efficient ways to study and learn.

The following informal survey will help you determine your natural global or analytic strengths. Later you will probably want to give this test to your child or to answer for him if he is too young to take it himself. Answer as honestly as possible, and even though you may want to choose both options on any given statement, always try to choose the one you would do *most* of the time.

What's My Dominant Learning Style?

Place a check mark beside the *one* statement in each pair that best describes your preferences *when you are learning.*

When you are learning, do you *usually:*

   A   B

1. __ like learning by yourself better than working with another person or group?
   __ like learning with another person or group better than working by yourself?

2. __ finish one job before going on to the next one?
   __ begin a new job even if you have not finished an earlier one?

3. __ begin your work without waiting to see how someone else does it?
   __ prefer to wait for someone else to start before you begin?

4. __ find it easier to remember details when you read than to remember main ideas?
   __ find it easier to remember main ideas when you read than to remember details?

5. __ prefer true-false and multiple choice tests with one right answer?
   __ prefer tests that ask you to explain reasons and write out answers?

6. __ need to have your desk and work area neat to concentrate?
   __ find you can get your work done even if your desk or work area is cluttered?

7. __ feel your time was wasted if the teacher doesn't put a grade on work you turned in?
   __ not mind the teacher not giving you a grade as long as your work was recognized?

8. __ prefer competing on your own to competing on a team?
   __ prefer competing on a team to competing on your own?

9. __ prefer to have choices as to how to accomplish assignments you're given?
   __ prefer that the teacher tells you exactly how the assignment should be done?

10. __ want to go over a test that's been graded in order to correct what you missed?
    __ want to look over your graded test but do not want to correct specific answers?

11. __ find it fairly easy to ignore distractions while you work or study?
    __ find it pretty difficult to ignore distractions while you work or study?

12. __ prefer to have an assignment in smaller parts and given step-by-step?
    __ need to know the whole assignment before you work on parts or steps?

13. __ prefer to think about a decision and figure out what to do by yourself?
    __ ask other people's opinions if you aren't sure about making a decision?

14. __ not take it personally if someone tells you you've done something wrong?
    __ automatically take it personally if someone says you've done something wrong?

15. __ blame the test if you don't do well and you studied what the teacher told you?
    __ blame yourself if you don't do well on a test and you studied what the teacher said?

__ __ **Column Totals**

Total the number of "check marks" in each column. If the number is greater in column A, you tend to be more *analytic*. If the number is greater in column B, you tend to be more *global*.

Although you got a higher number in one column, remember that there is no *pure* style. All of us are a mixture of *many* style characteristics. The terms *global* and *analytic* are extremes, and most of us will find ourselves to some extent in both categories. Remember, too, that how you came out on the Gregorc model will influence the type of global or analytic learner you are. For example, there's a big difference between an analytic who is Abstract Random and an analytic who is Concrete Sequential!

My husband, John, is extremely analytic by nature. When we watch a movie together, he must watch *every single* credit go by. He reads each name and notes each line of information. If you ask John later what the movie was about, he provides a *lengthy* retelling of the story, complete with snippets of dialogue. I watched the same movie. But because I am a more global learner, if you were to ask *me* what the movie was about, I would probably give you a very general and vague description of the plot. Who starred in the movie? I don't know—some tall guy with brown hair who plays on a TV show. Where was the movie filmed? I don't know—big city, tall buildings, snow on the ground. After all, you didn't tell me there was going to be a *quiz* at the end! You see, I just *experienced* the movie. I don't pay attention to specific details unless you tell me ahead of time what I'm supposed to be looking for.

The global learner sees the *big picture* or overall view, while the analytic focuses on the *parts* that make up the big picture. A more analytic learner figures you have to clearly understand the parts to eventually understand the whole. The more global learner claims there's no point in clarifying a detail if you can't see where it fits into the whole picture. The global sees all the parts as being related to each other and may have trouble breaking down the big picture into separate pieces.

It's a lot like putting together a jigsaw puzzle. As a global, I must constantly see the completed picture on the puzzle box to put the individual pieces together. My analytic husband often prefers to analyze how the shapes of the puzzle pieces fit together. He may put several sections of the puzzle together before he ever concerns himself with how everything fits into the completed picture.

Consider the following lists of characteristics for the analytic and the global learning styles. You'll probably identify with several items from *both* lists, but you may also discover a distinct pattern of preferences when it comes to how you approach and process what you need to know. Remember, this has to do *only* with how you interact with *information,* not necessarily how your global or analytic tendencies may show up in interpersonal relationships.

HOW ANALYTIC ARE YOU?

Analytic Strengths

- details
- focus
- organization
- remembering specifics
- direct answers
- consistency
- sense of justice
- objectivity
- individual competition
- doing one thing at a time

What You Should Know About the Analytic Style

- likes things ordered in a step-by-step way
- pays close attention to details
- must be prepared
- needs to know what to expect
- often values facts over feelings
- prefers to finish one thing at a time
- rarely becomes personally or emotionally involved
- logical
- self-motivated
- finds the facts but sometimes misses the main idea

Analytic Frustrations

- having opinion expressed as fact
- not understanding the purpose for doing something
- not understanding how a teacher grades
- listening to an overview without knowing the steps involved
- listening to an explanation when all that's needed is a "yes" or "no" answer
- dealing with generalities
- having to find personal meaning in all that they learn
- not finishing one task before going on to the next

HOW GLOBAL ARE YOU?

Global Strengths

- seeing the big picture
- seeing relationships
- cooperating in group efforts
- reading between the lines
- sense of fairness
- seeing many options
- paraphrasing
- doing several things at once
- giving and receiving praise
- reading body language
- getting others involved

What You Should Know About the Global Style

- sensitive to other people's feelings
- flexible
- goes with the flow
- learns by discussion and working with others
- needs reassurance and reinforcement
- works hard to please others
- takes all criticism personally
- avoids individual competition

- tries to avoid conflict
- may skip steps and details

Global Frustrations

- having to explain themselves analytically
- not getting a chance to explain themselves at all
- not knowing the meaning for doing something
- having to go step-by-step without knowing where they'll end up
- not being able to relate what they are learning to their own life
- not receiving enough credit for their effort
- having to show the steps they used to get an answer
- accepting criticism without taking it personally
- people who are insensitive to other people's feelings

Whether we are more global or analytic, we tend to assume that others want us to give them information in the same manner we ourselves would want to receive it.

In our home, John is by far more analytic than I, and I am frequently guilty of ignoring his need for specific information in favor of my more general outlook. A classic example is when he asked me where to find a particular item. "It's in the other room," I told him.

He just looked at me and blinked. "What other room?" he asked.

"The dining room."

"*Where* in the dining room?"

"The rolltop desk."

"*In* the rolltop desk or *on* it?"

"In it, I think."

"Toward the front or toward the back?"

"Toward the back."

"On the left or on the right?"

"On the left."

That incident happened a long time ago, and I've learned more about how an analytic mind expects to receive information. Now when John asks me where something is, I pause for a moment. Then I say something like, "It's in the kitchen in the cupboard to the left of the stove on the middle shelf toward the back on the right." He looks at me with a grateful smile and says, "*Thank you* for being so specific!"

Now I may not actually know where the item is, but I know it's close to the place I said. I have discovered that if I start out with very specific information, John doesn't mind continuing the search!

Since the Witkin model deals specifically with how we understand information, let's take a look at the differences between global and analytic learners when it comes to study skills.

PAYING ATTENTION

Your naturally dominant learning style affects how you listen, what you pay attention to, and what you remember.

When more global learners first hear new information, they take it in by listening for the "gist" of what's being said. They can quickly get the main idea or topic and may even find themselves getting ahead of the speaker. Because it is not natural for them to listen for specific *details*, it may sometimes appear that they haven't been paying attention at all. But they have been getting general impressions and an overall idea of what is being said. Unless more global learners consciously train themselves to listen for details, they may miss significant parts of assignments or lectures.

One mother asked her very global young daughter, "What did you do in school today?"

The daughter replied enthusiastically, "Oh, Mom, it was fun! We studied fractions. And the teacher drew a pizza, then it was a Mercedes sign, and then we all *ate* the pizza!"

Mom asked pleasantly, "Do you have any homework?"

Her daughter looked surprised. "Homework? I don't think so. I didn't hear the teacher say anything about homework."

This global child was so busy *experiencing* the class that little or no thought was given to a specific or bothersome detail like homework.

Let's look at the more analytic learner. When analytics first hear new information, they are usually listening for specific details. Later they may even be able to remember the exact words the speaker said. Since analytics naturally tune in to details, it's sometimes difficult for them to identify the overall *concept* the details are describing. For example, an analytic learner may be able to relate all the facts of a story just read but may not be able to explain the *theme*. The analytic must consciously stretch himself to see and understand the bigger picture.

FOLLOWING DIRECTIONS

The differences between the dominantly global and the dominantly analytic style are especially noticeable when it comes to listening and following directions. For example, when a parent or teacher gives directions, the analytic learner listens carefully, then wants to begin without further interruptions. The global learner may also listen to the directions, but he may frequently ask that the directions be repeated. The global was listening for *what* is supposed to be done, not necessarily *how to do it*. In addition, he is often distracted by wondering what *wasn't* said.

In a recent teaching strategies class, I divided the teachers into two groups—globals and analytics. Both groups were to design a lesson plan that would effectively teach extremely global students about Einstein's Special Theory of Relativity. Since some of the *teachers* were fuzzy about the theory, a physics teacher gave a quick 10-minute overview of it.

After the analytics had shared their detailed and comprehensive lesson plans, the globals got up to share theirs. They seemed a bit sheepish. The spokesperson said, "We have to admit we didn't really hear the explanation of the theory. While the physics teacher was explaining it, we kept thinking things like: *How did Einstein think of this? Where was his laboratory—in his garage? Was Einstein married? How did he find something that would go so fast?* By the time we had worked through those questions in our minds and had tuned in to what the speaker was saying, he was finished talking. We all had the sinking feeling that we were going to look dumb . . . again."

Analytic learners who are listening for details may become particularly frustrated if instructions are repeated. They are already focused on the task and do not want to have to again listen to something they already know. On the other hand, if globals are told there will be no repetition of the instructions and they have to get it the first time, they become particularly stressed because they know they probably won't be able to listen for everything at once.

How do you as a parent or teacher meet the needs of both analytic and global learners? Although there are no simple answers, if you make the general purpose clear before giving the *specifics*, you can often give directions without repetition. First tell us what we're going to do, then tell us how we're going to do it. For example, you may say something like, "We are going to study three major causes of the Civil War. You will need to identify two specific examples for each cause we discuss. Now, let me tell you where you can find these examples."

In some cases, if the process or concept being taught is complex, you simply have to encourage the analytics to have more tolerance for the globals. After all, if the globals didn't understand it the first time and the teacher doesn't repeat it, chances are it will be the analytic students next to these globals who will have to clarify what was said!

ORGANIZATION AND TIME MANAGEMENT

If you were speculating about the kind of learning style a person who teaches time management classes might be, which do you think it would be? You're right! Analytics! And who do you suppose *takes* these time management classes? Right again! Globals! Although both styles can be successfully organized, they usually have very different views of how organization and time management look. Is it any wonder that the standard methods employed in classrooms and at work so often don't work?

An extremely *analytic* English teacher insisted her high school students keep their papers in a three-ring binder under specific categories. Although most students complied, one boy, a true *global*, refused to bring a notebook with him every day. He always wore a military fatigue jacket with multiple pockets and was prepared with pens and paper. Finally, out of frustration with noncompliance, the teacher decided to do something about it.

One day, she stopped her students on the way out of class and told them they must all leave their notebooks on their desks. She would look at them that night and grade them according to whether all the papers were there and filed in the proper categories.

As each student placed a notebook on the desk, this particular boy shrugged off his coat, hung it on the back of his chair, and left. With a sinking feeling, the teacher checked the coat. Sure enough, each pocket was a category, and there wasn't a single paper missing!

It often makes the most sense to analytics to have a place for everything and everything in its place. Globals usually consider themselves organized if they are able to *find* something when they need it, even if they have to rummage through a whole pile of stuff to get it. Even though globals may not *appear* to be organized, you may be surprised at how quickly they can locate what they need.

Because the traditional school system is very analytically structured, the analytic learner's approach to managing time and materials fits and is greatly valued. The more global learners may struggle with organizing notebooks and materials enough to meet the grading requirements of a more analytic teacher. A global learning style often does not fit the traditional analytic school structure.

If you are the parent of a global child who seems to be constantly disorganized, try to help him understand the *need* to be organized. If the purpose of being organized is to be able to locate papers and materials later, your child needs to make sure his system (even if it looks pretty messy and disorganized to you) helps him do that. A good test is whether he can find any paper he needs in 60 seconds or less. If he can, obviously his system works, no matter how it looks. If he can't, his system needs to be improved.

When it comes to improving areas of time management and organization, globals and analytics struggle with different kinds of problems. On the following pages, you will find some of the most consistent areas of frustration for both styles and practical ways for dealing with those frustrations.

THE DOMINANT ANALYTIC

It's hard to work with interruptions. Because the natural bent of the dominant analytic mind is to learn by thinking about one thing at a time, it is very disruptive to his concentration to be focused on a concept or an idea, and then suddenly to have to think about something else. Consequently, the analytic is often much better off studying or working alone, then joining others for a social time *after* his work is done. If you, as a parent or teacher, think of something for the analytic to do or something you need to tell him before he finishes his current task, don't break his concentration by interrupting. Write it down and talk with him when he's finished.

There are too many places to organize at once. The dominant analytic is almost always more efficient when tasks or assignments can be divided into categories or pieces. For him, there is a much greater sense of accomplishment when he can make a big difference in a small place than when he is just barely making a small difference in a big place.

Just before our wedding several years ago, my global nature was running wild with random thoughts and last-minute tasks. I kept mentioning things to John, my analytic bridegroom. I'd say, "Don't forget you promised to mow the lawn before your mother arrives," and "Did you call that man about the contract negotiation?" and "Will you pick up the rings while you're in North Seattle?" Finally, John said, "Cindy, just make me a list." Well, I sat down and wrote out a beautiful "to do" list. I printed every item neatly, numbered each one, and put a space in front of each number so he could check it off after he had accomplished the task. I proudly presented my list, and John politely thanked me. A few minutes later as I walked through the dining room, I saw John sitting at the table recopying my list! "What's wrong with my list?" I asked.

He held up the piece of paper he was using to recopy the original list. The paper was neatly divided into four categories: "Personal," "Wedding," "Business," and "Miscellaneous." "You have everything clumped together on the same list," he replied a little incredulously. "You shouldn't have put contract negotiation (a necessary business task) and mowing the lawn (a nice thing to get done if there's time) on the same nonspecific list!" Once he had sorted my list, he began to work in earnest on accomplishing the tasks.

There needs to be some sort of system. The dominant analytic works best when there is a definite and consistent method of doing things, especially if he can create the system himself. Keeping a daily schedule and/or lists of things to do often helps the analytic keep a sense of structure and predictability. Analytics are usually most comfortable when they can set and meet specific goals, preferably on a daily basis.

THE DOMINANT GLOBAL

It's easier to get an organizational system than to keep it. Dominant globals often have what could be called a "pile and bulldoze" system of organizing papers and materials. They start out with all the best intentions of filing things away, but after they find and use something, they frequently toss it into a to-be-filed box, intending to put it where it belongs later. Before they know it, there is a huge pile of papers that practically needs to be bulldozed. A helpful tip is to simplify the system as much as possible so it will be easy for them to put things back. Big baskets or colorful files that hold very general categories of things will encourage at least getting papers back in the right area.

Once in awhile, even globals can become overwhelmed with lack of order. When I finally get to the point of actually cleaning and organizing my office, the first thing I do is take a trip to the store. I have a wonderful time shopping among the colored baskets, plastic drawers, and portable filing systems. When I get back to the office with my bounty, I'm usually out of the mood to organize, and I happily go back to work—in the chaos.

It's too easy to become distracted. The dominantly global mind seems to be going in many directions almost all the time. Just as the global is focused on one task, something else comes up that also has to be taken care of, and instead of finishing the first task, the global begins on the new one and works until something *else* distracts him from the previous task. One of the best ways to overcome this tendency to become distracted is to work with another person. You can promise to help each other finish one thing before going on to another. It's surprising how much easier it is to concentrate when someone else is working with you!

"I'll do it" doesn't always mean "I'll do it now." Often dominantly global students have the very best of intentions, but don't always follow through quickly enough for parents or teachers who have asked them to accomplish

a task. Procrastination is a real temptation for globals, and it can cause a lot of conflict with the analytics in their lives. If you want the global to do something *now*, try offering to work with him at least to get him started. For example, as a global, I often just need a "jump-start." If you will work alongside me even for a few minutes, the chances are very good that I will go ahead and complete the task.

GETTING THE BEST OF THE TEST

Although neither learning style necessarily *likes* tests, dominantly analytic students don't seem to feel as threatened or nervous about them as the more global students are. Dominantly global students usually take tests much more personally than their analytic classmates. Globals often believe that the teacher is out to trick them or make them feel dumb. To them the whole testing situation feels stiff and formal, and sometimes they do poorly on a test because they literally "psyche" themselves into failing.

Dominant analytic students, on the other hand, seem to approach tests with more confidence. Because the analytic nature automatically breaks down information into component parts, the analytic student has an easier time dividing a test into manageable pieces. If the analytic dreads a test, it's usually because he is not prepared and not because he feels the teacher is out to get him.

One of the biggest frustrations for globals is that they understand the whole concept but struggle with the specific and objective testing techniques that seem to suit analytics perfectly. If globals can gain more confidence in nitty-gritty test-taking skills, they will find they are much smarter than their test scores show.

Both my sister Sandee and I are global. We were talking to a physics teacher when Sandee brought up an interesting question. "If a microwave oven can make things *hot* fast, why can't they invent something that would make things *cold* fast?" The teacher smiled indulgently and stated that it was against the laws of physics. He then patiently defined and explained the law. When he finished, Sandee echoed the question on my mind. "OK, but if a microwave oven can make things *hot* fast . . ." His definition had just sped over the top of our heads!

My husband, who is a great interpreter in such matters, stepped in. "It's like this," he explained. "Suppose you had 1,000 ping-pong balls in a net, and the net was tied to the ceiling. If you released the net, the ping-pong balls would quickly spread all over the room. That's the concept behind the microwave. In order to *reverse* the process, you'd have to gather up all the ping-pong balls, put them back in the net, and reattach it to the ceiling."

Got it. I still couldn't tell you what the law is called or take a test on it to save my life, but I understand the concept of how it works. Unfortunately for us globals, we rarely get credit in school for understanding a global concept if we can't pass a test on the analytic details.

I recently asked several groups of teenage students to give me some test-taking tips. Although the analytic groups began serious consideration right away, the globals first listed items like "Lose a contact so you can't take the test," "Stage a fire drill," and "Get a paper cut and bleed on the test so your teacher will feel sorry for you."

After some discussion, the analytic and global students who have successfully coped with all sorts of tests shared some of their secrets. It won't be hard to see the difference between these two lists!

Test Tips from Dominant Analytic Students

- Scan the test quickly to see how many essay, multiple choice, and true-false questions you'll have to answer. Then divide your time according to how long you have to take the test.
- Do the easy questions first; skip the ones that look hard or complex and come back to them later.
- Keep your desk or work area completely clear of clutter; it will help you concentrate during the test.
- Always have an extra pen or pencil during the test.

Test Tips from Dominant Global Students

- Dress comfortably the day of the test.
- Eat something before the test so you won't feel hungry.
- After you have studied for the test, get together with a small group of classmates and review by testing each other.

• Don't come to class too early the day of a test or you may get confused by all the last-minute cramming.

During a short presentation at a youth conference, I noticed a seventh-grade girl listening intently and enthusiastically to everything I said about learning styles and study skills. When the session was over, she bolted out the door and I heard her yell to her friend, "Hey, Stacy! I'm not dumb—I'm *global!*"

FIGURING OUT TEACHERS

No teacher is going to be *just* global or *just* analytic. But it is often helpful for students to look at certain teacher behaviors and preferences. It may help them understand why they are experiencing frustration in those teachers' classrooms.

Parents and students might think it would be best for the teacher and student to have the same dominant learning style. However, this is not necessarily the case. Sometimes, the best situation is for a more global student to be in an analytic teacher's classroom. The analytic teacher can give the global student much-needed structure; and sometimes an analytic student does best in a global teacher's classroom because, there, he can get the big picture rather than just focusing on details.

Since most teachers will be a *mix* of global and analytic behaviors and preferences, it is important to recognize which learning style demands the teacher is making of his students. Understanding what the teacher expects from students is more important than trying to figure out the teacher's dominant style. To help you identify which learning style your child's teacher demands, here are five basic areas where the global or analytic expectations are evident.

Classroom Environment

You can often determine whether a teacher is more global or more analytic just by looking at his classroom. A global teacher may have a classroom that is designed to look like a home away from home. There are posters, plants, rugs, and couches. To the analytic that may look like a whole lot of junk. But to the global, it's "atmosphere."

An analytic teacher's room may look pretty bare by contrast. When you walk into the analytic teacher's classroom, you may find fire drill instructions, daily announcements, and charts and graphs relevant to the day's lesson. Anything else would be considered a distraction. Analytic teachers often keep their classrooms as clean and organized as possible so that the student can concentrate on learning and not the environment.

During a summer class for teachers, one analytic teacher admitted that she was completely prepared for the next fall. She had, in fact, layered her bulletin board so that each month would already be posted. She was soundly "booed" by the globals!

Classroom Organization

Teachers with a strong analytic style will almost always have a set of classroom rules printed and distributed to students at the beginning of the year. The rules, as well as the consequences, are stated specifically so there won't be any confusion.

More global teachers will simply have one or two general classroom rules. For example, "Be kind and courteous to everyone" or "Respect others." Then, when other situations come up requiring the application of specific rules, a global teacher simply handles the problems on a case-by-case basis.

Attitude Toward Students

Global teachers place a high priority on self-esteem and will even teach lessons on self-esteem before they teach their subject matter. The global teacher is convinced that students cannot be successful unless they first have confidence in themselves.

Now, analytic teachers *also* believe that self-esteem is important, but they believe that you achieve self-esteem by experiencing success. So dominantly analytic teachers may set high standards and may seem to be hard on their students because they want the student to succeed in order to gain self-esteem.

Sometimes it's hard for global students to feel that an analytic teacher cares very much about them. In reality both analytic and global teachers can have equal amounts of compassion, but it is just expressed in different ways.

Suppose an important faculty meeting is scheduled at 3:00 P.M. At 2:55, an analytic teacher is rounding the corner, headed for the door of the meeting room. A distraught student intercepts him and asks for help. Chances are good that the analytic teacher will pause, calm the student as much as possible, then set a time to meet with the student later, either after the meeting or before school the next morning.

Now, let's say that the same distraught student intercepts a *global* teacher five minutes before the meeting starts. Chances are better than not that the global teacher will never make it to the meeting. Does either teacher care more? No. Both teachers have compassion but each expresses it in a different way.

Teaching the Content

When it comes to teaching the content of a lesson, more analytic teachers use a lot of lectures, individual activities, and reading projects. They encourage students to work independently and may sometimes appear almost unfriendly to global students.

A more global teacher tends to use discussion, group activities, and cooperative learning. Since global teachers seek to make the subject matter personally important to every student, they often share personal experiences and expect their students to do the same. This can make an analytic very uncomfortable or impatient.

Grading Practices

Analytic teachers almost always have a set grading scale. If 92-100 points is an A and a student gets 91.8 points, an analytic teacher will give the student a B. Dominant analytic teachers often have very specific grading criteria, and the student can count on that teacher to be consistent. Analytic teachers may appear not to give out many compliments, but when that teacher says "good," it may very well be the highest praise you'll receive from him or her!

Global teachers don't like to be very specific with grades. If 92 is an A and a student gets 91.8, the global teacher may say, "Close enough," depending on how hard the teacher believes the student worked. Dominantly global teachers emphasize class participation and may even grade on how often contributions are made to class discussions or group work. Global teachers will usually give their students a lot of positive feedback, complimenting them on things that may not have anything to do with their classroom work.

Parents and students need to understand that *every* style of teacher can contribute a great deal to a student's success. The key to achieving success is how well students understand what the teacher is doing or is asking them to do.

We cannot put people in boxes and say everyone is just like everyone else who has the same learning style. We do people a terrible injustice when we categorize them. A CS, an AS, an AR, or a CR may have all of the characteristics we attribute to those categories and yet may be very global, or at the other extreme, very analytic.

This can be confusing and may not seem to fit. We may not think a CS with a global way of thinking is a possibility. But it happens. It is also possible for an AR to have a strong analytic side.

Because you are not just a "pure" learning style, add to your picture what you might find in the room that would indicate you are a global or an analytic. Look at our example of a global AR to get some ideas.

In a Nutshell

Understanding information is fundamental to almost everything we do on a day-to-day basis. Knowing if we naturally understand information analytically or globally can help us step outside our dominant style and use a completely different style. Understanding that we can make this switch is especially valuable in an academic setting. It is equally important in the areas of business and communication in general. If I don't understand what you mean, how can I know what you're saying?

Chapter Ten

How Many Ways Can We Be Smart?

Do you feel smart?

How do you even know whether or not you *are* smart?

Who *decides*, anyway?

For generations, parents have been led to believe they should use IQ tests to determine where to place their children in school or what kind of programs might be most appropriate. If you've been reading this book in sequence, you've probably already discovered that intelligence comes in *all* styles. It doesn't even *look* the same in all styles. We've been trained as parents and teachers to value the limited kind of intelligence that conforms to a traditional school system's style of learning: logic and mathematical skills, verbal and written communication skills, and analytical and organizational abilities. If you or your child happens to be smart in a way that isn't measured or valued in school, you get the idea that others are smarter and more successful than you are. *But that just isn't true!*

Several years ago, Howard Gardner, a Harvard professor and eminent researcher, released compelling evidence that each human being possesses *many* intelligences. Each of those intelligences appears to be housed in a different part of the brain. So far, Dr. Gardner has been able to identify seven, and he's still working on discovering others.

Educators, realizing the importance of this research, are beginning to adopt a multifaceted model for schools that incorporates the multiple intelligences. When it is adopted, Dr. Gardner's model will make a profound difference in the restructuring of public schools in America. Instead of rote drill and repetition of facts, the multiple intelligence approach helps children experience learning by gaining hands-on experience through apprenticeships. Instead of simply memorizing facts about civil wars and conflicts, students gain an understanding of why wars happen in the first place and what can be done to prevent them. Without compromising academic outcomes, the multiple intelligence model can help students succeed in learning by identifying and using their natural intelligence strengths to cope with almost any task.

This chapter contains a brief overview of this important research. For a more thorough grasp, read Howard Gardner's book *Frames of Mind* and Thomas Armstrong's book *7 Kinds of Smart* (see bibliography).

Unlike other learning style traits we have discussed, Gardner's research claims that intelligence is not fixed at birth, nor does it remain consistent throughout a lifetime. It grows, changes, and develops with the passing of time and with the opportunities afforded the individual. Parents and educators need to recognize and appreciate as many different areas of intelligence as possible within each child. Standard IQ tests may measure how well a person is likely to perform in the current, traditional school system, but the tests do not even come close to predicting a child's potential for success in life after he leaves school.

The principal of a private school recently admitted to me that the administration loves the traditional, sequential, well-behaved students. "But," she confided, "we're very *nice* to those students who struggle with school, because they are often the ones who end up making lots of money and later come back to endow the school!"

According to Gardner's findings, everyone can develop a reasonable use of all seven intelligences, although the chances are good that each person tends to shine in two or three and must struggle to become more adept in the others. As you look through the brief descriptions, you will probably have no trouble identifying those that come easily for you. Regardless of what you may have been taught, any or *all* of these intelligences indicate that you are smart. And remember, no one has to be good at *everything*!

Linguistic

Linguistic intelligence has to do with verbal abilities, and those who possess great amounts of this kind of intelligence tend to be very good at writing, reading, speaking, and debating. Many journalists, teachers, and poets find themselves gifted with a high degree of linguistic intelligence. Because conventional IQ tests place a great deal of value on linguistic abilities, a person who is linguistically inclined usually is considered to be very smart. The more linguistic person often has and uses an extensive vocabulary and tends to be particularly skilled with word games and semantics.

My husband John is highly linguistic. He uses language very literally and chooses his words carefully when speaking. Early in our dating relationship, we had an argument. I am not very good at apologizing, but in one of my rarer moments, I swallowed my pride and gulped out the words "I'm sorry." He calmly turned to me and said, "*Sorry* is a statement of condition; *apologize* is the active verb. Now are you sorry, or do you apologize?" Although *no* more words were exchanged *that* evening, I had come to realize the importance he placed on phrasing!

Just because you may not be gifted linguistically doesn't mean you can't develop enough linguistic skills to survive and conquer the challenges of a society who values them. In Armstrong's book *7 Kinds of Smart*, you will find a list of ways you can deliberately develop linguistic as well as the other intelligences.

Logical-Mathematical

Logical-mathematical intelligence has to do with an individual's abilities in numbers, patterns, and logical reasoning. Although I have to admit the very *thought* of this intelligence makes me break out in a cold sweat, I do believe everyone needs to possess at least a basic understanding of the tenets of math and logic. Certainly if the logical-mathematical comes easily for you, you should score high on traditional IQ tests. Those who are naturally gifted in logical-mathematical intelligence are often the greatest scientists, mathematicians, and philosophers. On a more practical basis, you need logical-mathematical intelligence to successfully cope with balancing a checkbook or grasping the significance of the national debt.

My more logical and sequential friends are usually horrified to find I don't balance my checkbook. I *do* call the toll-free number periodically to make sure I'm in the ballpark, and I never have bounced a check, but I have real difficulty with the detailed reconciliation on my bank statement. On the other hand, my mother-in-law balances her bank statement *immediately* upon receipt. For me it's more practical to simply switch banks every couple years and get a fresh start!

It is important to recognize that logical-mathematical intelligence doesn't mean you have to be a math whiz. So much of our lives are involved with the mysteries of the scientific universe that most of us don't even realize how much logical-mathematical intelligence we already use. Maybe if we can stop thinking about numbers and logic in cold impersonal terms, we can make them more appealing for everyone.

Spatial

Spatial intelligence gives you the ability to think in vivid mental pictures, re-creating or restructuring a given image or situation. Those who are gifted spatially can often look at something and instantly pinpoint areas that could be changed to improve or alter its appearance. Highly spatial professions include architecture, drafting, and mechanical drawing. In almost any given situation, those with spatial intelligence have the natural ability to see what something *could* be as easily as what it is.

My statistics professor in college, a man highly gifted spatially, insists that he is a basically an *intuitive* person. "For example," he said, "when I drive to a place I've never been before, I look at a map and memorize it visually. As I head to my destination, I mentally bring up the map and 'intuitively' drive right to it."

For those of us who are not as gifted spatially, it is easy to recognize that this professor's skill in locating his destination has little to do with intuition. It is his acute spatial ability that allows him to visually re-create an accurate map in his mind's eye.

You might recognize a spatial exercise on a standard IQ test as one of those cubes flattened out, with your task being to state which side will be on top when the cube is reconstructed. Does this look familiar?

These squares will fold into a box which is open at the top. Which letter would mark the BOTTOM of the box?

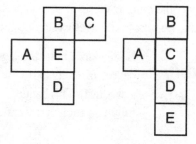

Don't let it make you feel less smart if you can't automatically see the relationships!

Musical

Musical intelligence expresses itself through a natural rhythm and melody, and one who is gifted in this area often seems to live as if life is set to music. Although you may not have "an ear for music" or "perfect pitch," you can still possess a great deal of inherent musical appreciation ability. Many people need music in the background when they are working, and they find themselves tapping their feet almost subconsciously. If you are high in musical intelligence, you may listen to music more analytically than most, appreciating the nuances others may miss altogether.

Cathy, a young mother, told me that she felt at a distinct disadvantage with her 10-year-old daughter, Michelle. "Although we're both musically inclined," Cathy said, "Michelle tends to be too analytic for me to really enjoy listening to a performance with her. As we're listening to a classical piece, she'll pause and say, 'There—listen. Do you hear that French horn?' As I'm struggling to pick it out, she's already identifying a 'really cool bass guitar bridge.' And I thought it just sounded like a nice song!"

Many children are drawn to music and are eager to try their hand at a musical instrument at home or school. Unfortunately when a school district must make budget cuts, one of the first programs to go is the music program. There are many ways we can incorporate musical abilities into our homes and classrooms, and if we can become more effective in our efforts to build on our children's musical strengths, we may find ourselves singing their praises!

Bodily-Kinesthetic

Bodily-kinesthetic intelligence reflects a high degree of ability in bodily movement or physical activity. This includes those who can skillfully use their hands, such as surgeons or mechanics; those who so beautifully bring art to life, such as actors, actresses, and artists; and those who vigorously pursue a blend of physical activity and mental strategies, such as athletes and coaches. Although schools are highly enthusiastic about physical education and sports activities, the bodily-kinesthetic intelligence is not often valued as a way of being smart. In fact, sometimes a gifted athlete who can't be as successful linguistically as another student is accused of being a "dumb jock." It's time we recognize and value kinesthetic intelligence instead of considering only quiet academic intelligence an indicator of accomplishment.

Two adult sisters came to me after a seminar I had given on the subject of multiple intelligences. They had tears in their eyes as they related the story of their dad, who had dropped out of school in the eighth grade and had gone on to earn a living as a woodworker. His cabinetry and furniture was absolutely flawless and in great demand. Even though his workmanship shows great kinesthetic intelligence, he has always felt inadequate. His self-esteem has suffered for years, because he is convinced that it is not possible to be smart if you didn't successfully complete school.

The bodily-kinesthetic person can often "feel things in their bones," and their lives are full of physical activity. The more we try to force these folks to sit still, the more restless their minds become and the less effective formal instruction can be. Instead of fighting their need to move, we need to find ways to channel this energy into positive learning.

Interpersonal

Interpersonal intelligence affords those who have it the gift of understanding, appreciating, and getting along well with other people. This intelligence is not usually measured in the traditional academic setting, and those who possess it often find themselves in trouble for using it! These people have a sixth sense when it comes to reading another person. They can almost always tell when something's wrong, even if no words have been spoken. Those who need a friend are quickly drawn to the person with interpersonal intelligence.

One teacher admitted she did not keep traditional lesson plans. Her lesson plan book was, in fact, more of a *diary* where she recorded what she did, not what she planned. She had a general idea of what needed to be communicated, but she would wait to "get a sense" of where the students were on any given day before she determined how to proceed with the lesson.

Many of those in the helping professions such as counseling or ministry find themselves relying heavily upon their interpersonal abilities for success in their careers. Although you can work on developing this intelligence, it seems many remain very uncomfortable if they are not naturally gifted interpersonally.

Intrapersonal

Intrapersonal intelligence is not always readily apparent in a person because it so often expresses itself in solitude. It is a natural gift of understanding ourselves, knowing who and what we are, and how we fit into the greater scheme of the universe. Those who are naturally strong intrapersonally enjoy times of reflection, meditation, and time alone. They seem to possess a more positive self concept than most, and they don't rely on others' opinions to determine their life goals and aspirations.

A perfect example of intrapersonal intelligence is found in the book *The Accidental Tourist* by Anne Tyler. The main character, Macon, said of a woman friend that she talked too much. Macon, on the other hand, was the kind of man who thought silence was better than music. When his wife would switch off the radio, he'd say, "Listen! They're playing my song."

Sometimes we misunderstand those who excel in intrapersonal intelligence. We may accuse them of being introverted and shy, when those characteristics may actually be indicative of great inner strength.

In a Nutshell

No single test can ever measure or predict a person's intelligence. Everyone can win when given a chance to show *how* they are smart. The acceptance of a theory about multiple intelligences helps us value the differences among various world cultures. Although our culture may place a high value on linguistic intelligence, in some areas of the world, one's ability to read and write would take a back seat to spatial skills if you needed to navigate the seas to survive. The more we learn to identify and use multiple ways of being smart, the more effective our education system can become in equipping the next generation for dealing with the real world.

Chapter Eleven

Putting It All Together

I had just finished teaching two days of intensive learning and communicating styles training for a large police department. The police chief called me into his office to express his appreciation and to make an important request. He handed me a list of all his employees by name, including police officers, clerks, and other staff. "I'd like you to put each person's learning style category in the space beside his name," he said matter of factly.

I tried to hide the dismay I felt at his cut-and-dried categorization. However, I knew how *his* learning styles assessments had come out. So I said, "OK, let's start with *your* name. What style category should I put beside it?"

He thought for a moment. "I came out AR," he replied, "but actually, my CS was only a couple of points behind. And, truthfully, I am more analytic than global. And I'm definitely more visual."

I smiled. "So what shall I write beside your name?"

141

He frowned uncomfortably, then sighed. "OK, OK, I get your point. No *one* category can really describe anyone. But it would be so easy if I could just keep a file in my desk that lets me instantly figure out what style I'm dealing with!"

When we first discover this whole area of learning styles, there is a tendency to label everyone and everything according to one particular style, to categorize or put them in a box. But the more you understand about learning styles, the less you will try to categorize yourself and others. Each person is as unique as his or her fingerprints. Although many fingerprints may look basically the same, no one pattern is exactly like another. Sometimes the differences are hard to notice; at other times, they are quite obvious.

In this book, I have introduced you to five different learning styles models to help you understand that each person is a complex and unique combination of natural strengths and preferences. Let's quickly list them for review:

Mind-styles (Gregorc)

Recognizing how the mind works.

Environmental Preferences (Dunn and Dunn)

Designing the ideal study environment.

Modalities (Barbe-Swassing)

Learning strategies for remembering.

Analytic/Global Information Processing (Witkin)

Identifying effective methods of learning and study skills.

Multiple Intelligences (Gardner)

Identifying seven different areas of intelligences.

Each of these learning styles adds another dimension to our insights about ourselves and others in our families. In addition to these, there are literally hundreds of learning style models. The five I have chosen to share with you are my favorites, because I have seen firsthand how accurate and practical the results of these models can be, and because each has an extremely reliable research base. Now that you have become aware of these learning styles, you will encounter other means of identifying styles. Consider each model or test to be another layer of understanding and not a replacement for the labels you already know.

For many of us, no matter how many learning style assessments we take, we find our natural strengths and preferences to be very consistent with one another. For example, my random nature lives with my global style quite compatibly. I don't struggle to understand who I am or what I need in most situations. The obvious drawback to this consistency is that when I need to use the characteristics that are *opposite* my natural strengths, it takes a good deal of discipline and hard work, and I am left feeling frustrated and exhausted.

One of my best friends finds herself strongly random, but she is also very analytical. This causes her a great deal of conflict within herself. She needs structure and specific facts for analytic learning, but as a random communicator, she fights regimentation and detail. Once she began to understand about learning styles, she could use her seemingly contradictory traits to bring balance to her life. She practiced using her analytical side when she needed to be specific and switched to her random side when she needed to see the big picture.

Some people are frustrated that they never seem to fall into *any* definite category on any learning or communicating styles assessments. I usually suggest, lightheartedly, that they are either very well balanced or *really* mixed up! They are willing to admit they feel mixed up, but with a little more knowledge about and practice of learning styles, they usually begin to see the advantage of switching easily from style to style as circumstances dictate.

One of the most important things to remember about learning styles is that they are *value neutral*. There is no one best style to be. No single style is any smarter than another, nor is there any style combination that is automatically good or naturally bad. The key lies in how you *use* your natural style strengths, and in how willing you are to learn or communicate in a way that may be difficult for you.

USING LEARNING STYLES TO SURVIVE AND CONQUER!

Over my years of teaching learning styles to virtually all kinds of audiences, I have discovered a very consistent pattern in successfully understanding and using learning styles concepts and strategies. Both children and adults experience five stages in coming to fully understand them.

Stage One—Awareness

When we first discover the differences between the dominant learning styles perspectives, we enter the stage of awareness. There are a lot of "ah-ha's!" and enlightening revelations, and it is usually fun just to revel in being the "real" us. For many, it is both reassuring and, at the same time, unsettling to think that others actually *do* perceive the world as we do! Children who find learning difficult are especially delighted and encouraged to discover they are smart and capable after all, and they are usually eager to talk about what they like and how they learn best.

Stage Two—Opposite Camps

After the initial joy of discovery, the next stage can cause concern to those around us. When we look at the characteristics of those whose dominant style is opposite ours, we may decide our style is better than theirs. Without meaning to, we may even go so far as to insult those who are in opposite style groups.

Since children sometimes have a tendency to exaggerate the differences, adults may become alarmed when they hear the dominant globals or randoms referred to as "space cadets," or the dominant analytics or sequentials dubbed as "uptight nerds." A wise parent intervenes with gentle and consistent reminders that there is no best style, and each person's strengths are needed to keep the world in balance. This negative stage is just a normal part of the process of understanding learning styles. Fortunately, it doesn't last long.

Stage Three—Appreciation

After we have determined that we *like* our own natural style, we begin to realize some of our limitations. At that point, we come to appreciate the dominant styles that are opposite ours. We discover firsthand that each style has its strengths, and we can benefit from *all* of them. For example, when the more global students have been absent for two or three days and need to get notes or homework assignments from other students, it isn't a global classmate they ask for information. As much as they *like* their global friends, they search out their more *analytic* classmates who probably wrote down the assignment word for word and know every detail.

By the same token, dominant analytics often don't want to work in groups where everyone is analytic. For one thing, it seems that analytics often don't take into consideration how other people feel. They are all so interested in getting their point across that they are not always paying attention to how others are responding. Another problem with an all-analytic group is that nobody looks at the big picture They are all caught up in the details. Pretty soon participants are looking around saying, "We'd better find a couple of globals for our group." This is the appreciation stage in action, and it is where children and adults alike can begin to see that other styles have a lot to offer.

The Fourth Stage—Excuses

After the positive stage of learning to appreciate other styles comes a stage that is perhaps the hardest for parents and teachers to tolerate. They hear children say things like: "I'm a random—I don't do math," or "I'm analytic—I don't do groups."

Again, it is necessary to give firm, loving reminders that if we are using our learning style simply as an excuse, we have not yet learned how to use it to succeed. When we discover our strengths, we can then *use* them to conquer virtually *anything*. And once we've learned how to use our strengths to succeed, we will no longer *need* excuses!

Stage Five—Style Flex

Style flex happens when we can take our natural style strengths and consciously flex or bend them into other learning styles that don't make as much sense to us or are not as comfortable for us. It can be done and it's something we do on purpose. You may be surprised at how much easier it is to do a task that is opposite from what is natural for you when you can identify which parts cause the problem. At that point you can *deliberately* set out to overcome the difficulties.

Parents encounter the most resistance from children who do not understand *why* they are being asked to learn in a way that does not make sense to them. When forced to step out of their natural style even before they understand or accept what their own style *is*, they feel frustrated and inferior because they do not experience success. Once children are given the opportunity to identify and use their inherent learning style strengths, they begin to feel confident enough in their abilities to stretch out of their comfort zones and attempt tasks that are more difficult.

HELPING YOUR CHILD SUCCEED IN THE CLASSROOM

Sometimes parents feel strongly that their children would learn best if they were taught by teachers who shared the same basic learning style strengths. However, it may actually be better to learn from a teacher who presents information from an entirely different perspective. For example, a global teacher may give a broader view to an analytic child. A sequential teacher may bring order to a random-style learner.

There's no question about it—children must learn to get along with *many* different kinds of learning styles if they want to be successful in our diverse and changing world. What's important to remember is that your child must *want* to learn to get along with different styles and approaches. That motivation will be different for each child.

When speaking to students, I often try to illustrate the importance of accommodating styles other than their own so they will not be limited in their success. Here is one of those illustrations that seems to demonstrate the importance of accommodation:

Suppose you were going to live in a foreign country for two years. You don't plan to learn the language, and you plan to talk only to those who can speak English. Furthermore, you have no plans to change your life-style by adapting to native customs and habits. You've made up your mind to do only what is comfortable for you.

Now you could probably *survive*, but you're not going to have the same kind of experience that you could have if you were to take the time and effort to learn the native language and life-styles of the country. The same is true for you at school, at home, and later in your career. By learning to adapt to other styles, you will broaden your scope of influence and success.

In a Nutshell

One learning style can be almost as different from another as two foreign languages are from each other. As parents and teachers, if we can become "multilingual" in styles, we can teach our children to value many different perspectives without sacrificing their own. But most importantly, we can help our children be successful in *spite* of school and workplace systems as well as because of them.

Chapter Twelve

The Difference Between Learning Style and Learning Disability

Karen was a lively, mischievous first grader when her teacher and principal began to suggest that her parents have her screened for possible hyperactivity or Attention Deficit Disorder (A.D.D.). Even though Karen was bright and creative, they explained, she simply didn't follow directions. She was often restless and had difficulty staying at a task for more than five minutes at a time. She rarely completed written assignments, and her social interactions with her classmates were frequently immature and moody.

Karen's parents took her to a pediatrician. Subsequently, she went through an intensive screening process to determine whether or not she had a learning disability. The results of the testing led the doctor to conclude that Karen, indeed, had a marginal case of A.D.D. It was recommended that Karen begin a mild dose of medication to control her behavior.

Karen's parents and grandparents were troubled at the prospect of putting their bright, cheerful, six year old on serious and regular medication. They began to explore other alternatives, and in the process, they heard about learning styles and how they affect study habits and behavior. As they began to understand Karen's natural learning style, they realized the way in which Karen learned was often not compatible with classroom demands.

For example, Karen is a very kinesthetic learner who thrives on movement combined with listening. The teacher wanted her to sit still. But her parents decided to try another approach. Instead of forcing Karen to be still and look at them when they were giving her directions, they decided to let her fidget, squirm, and look around. Then they checked to see if she had been listening and were amazed to find she could repeat what they had said almost word for word.

Karen's global nature made it possible for her to continually scan the environment, listening and paying attention to multiple voices and stimuli. Her dominantly random mind was constantly searching for alternatives and seeing possibilities not obvious to most people. Her CR characteristics made her very impatient when learning anything that didn't immediately interest her.

Her parents also discovered some emotional problems that seemed to explain Karen's sometimes immature behavior with her friends and classmates. These were addressed. Then, by helping Karen come to terms with her natural learning strengths, her parents and teacher helped her overcome many of her frustrations with the traditional classroom and learning demands. They didn't let Karen give up when something didn't make sense to her, and they encouraged her to use what came naturally to her. They challenged her to find ways she *could* be successful.

Karen's parents were wise in that they explored many alternatives for solving her difficulties with school. They made medication a last resort and not a quick fix. Although many children *do* benefit from a regimen of medication, I am encountering many teachers, physicians, and learning specialists who are concerned that far too many children are being rapidly and inappropriately labeled with A.D.D. or another disability and are being placed on medication too quickly.

Many students who are struggling in school simply have learning styles that are incompatible with the structure of the traditional classroom and academic demands. Sometimes concerned parents jump to a conclusion and believe their children may have learning disabilities or disorders of some kind because they lack success in school. To help their children succeed, parents can spend an inordinate amount of money and energy searching for programs and cures. What they need to do is take time to sort out how much of the problem might be attributable to an incompatibility of the child's learning style with the school's traditional method of teaching

Remember that a typical school classroom makes very definite learning style demands. A student is required to sit still (very difficult for the kinesthetic learner), learn quietly (not always easy for the auditory learner who needs to hear it aloud), work independently (often counter productive for the globals and ARs), and demonstrate knowledge sequentially (very frustrating for randoms and globals).

For children who possess learning styles that match academic demands, school does not normally present much of a problem. But when students find themselves at odds with school, they can become frustrated with both themselves and the system. Without a knowledge and understanding of learning styles, students often can't tell a teacher what works for them and what is difficult, nor can they develop effective strategies for coping with the opposite styles of either the teacher or the classroom.

There are more dimensions to consider. Many problems are beyond the scope of simple learning styles. Such things as family dysfunction, violence, emotional disorders, physical limitations, or chemical imbalance can affect a child's ability to learn. Often these problems require the service of medical and professional people and agencies. It is surprising to find out how much more effective the intervention of these professionals will be when we can identify the dominant learning styles of those who are *experiencing* the problems.

It is important to understand that even the best programs and approaches can work *backwards* if there isn't a significant match between the learning styles of the child and the style of the program designed to help him. If you can help your children discover and use methods that work *with* their natural style strengths instead of against them, you may find them succeeding more than you ever thought possible.

After reading this book, you already know a lot more about the individual learning styles of your children. But if you find your child in need of professional intervention, you can begin to ask some important questions of those who offer programs to help him or her. If you know your child is more sequential, does the program offer a simple, logical structure? If your child is random, does the program offer flexibility and a personal approach?

In my work with pediatricians and learning specialists, I have found the most effective professionals are those who are committed to a balanced approach when dealing with learning difficulties. This approach takes into consideration a child's dominant learning styles as well as other factors such as mental, emotional, or physical disabilities.

Physical limitations do exist in some children, and I am grateful we have so many well-qualified and dedicated specialists to diagnose and treat these ailments. I would, however, encourage parents of struggling children to take down the lines of first defense. Before we take any drastic actions or interventions, we need to devote time and energy toward really getting to know and understand our children as individuals. We must not be too quick in assuming that the child's misbehavior or annoying habits are symptoms of a learning disorder. Sometimes we, parents, focus on how we would like our children to *act* more than what we want our children to *accomplish*. But if we focus more on *outcomes* and less on *methods*, we may find our children succeeding in ways that have never occurred to us. As you define what you are trying to get the child to do or learn—the desired result—and not on the process by which he learns, you may discover some very reasonable alternatives to traditional approaches.

Here are just a few examples of troublesome behaviors that often give parents reason to believe their child has a learning problem, when actually the behaviors may be an indication of learning styles that are incompatible with the demands being made.

The Problem

The child is restless; he will not sit still.

What Do You Need to Accomplish?

I need for him to listen attentively to the story being read.

An Alternative

Give him the option of sitting on the floor or changing positions discreetly, as long as he does not distract those around him. Hold him accountable for being able to relate the facts or main idea of the story.

What Do You Need to Accomplish?

I need for him to understand the concept being taught.

An Alternative

Have him explain the concept to a parent, a teacher, or a classmate, either verbally or in written form.

What Do You Need to Accomplish?

I need for him to follow verbal directions.

An Alternative

Have him repeat back what he heard to check his understanding of the directions.

What Do You Need to Accomplish?

I need for him to not distract the other children around him.

An Alternative

Challenge him to come up with creative ways to move around without bothering anyone. For example, could he doodle, take notes, move his feet quietly?

Combining the Alternatives for a Restless Child

A primary teacher found out for herself how much difference it could make in classroom management if she simply defined her outcomes. She had been struggling with a fidgety, strong-willed boy who refused to sit in his seat and listen to the story she was reading. In frustration, she stopped for a moment and asked herself, "What's the point? What do I need to accomplish here? Do I need him to sit in this chair, or do I need him to listen to the story?" She then gave him the option of sitting anywhere he wanted as long as he listened quietly to the story and did not disturb others around him. To her amazement, he immediately complied by sitting in the back of the room on the floor and giving her his full attention.

The Problem

The child will not complete assignments.

What Do You Need to Accomplish?

I need for him to finish what he starts.

An Alternative

Help him break up the assignment into smaller, more manageable pieces. Don't insist that the whole task be done in one sitting, but hold him accountable for all the parts.

What Do You Need to Accomplish?

I need for him to prove he knows the material.

An Alternative

Challenge him that if he can maintain a minimum score (i.e. 92 or higher) on each test, he only has to do as much of each homework assignment he feels is necessary to master the concept.

Combining the Alternatives for Getting a Child to Complete Assignments

Sarah was a bright, capable fifth grader who, after excelling in math during the first half of the year, suddenly decided to quit doing her math homework. Sarah's teacher and parents were concerned. Homework counted for a substantial portion of the semester grade, and now Sarah's normally excellent grade point average seemed to be in jeopardy.

I was called in to talk to Sarah to discover what might have caused this abrupt change in her behavior, as well as what might motivate her to start turning in her homework again. It didn't take long for Sarah to tell me why she no longer did her homework.

"It's too boring," she explained simply. "I hate having to do 20 problems when I understand how to do the process after doing five of them. I just decided it wasn't worth the trouble."

"Can you pass the math tests without any trouble?" I asked.

"Oh, sure," she replied. "I always get As on my tests."

After some discussions with Sarah, her parents, and her teacher, we came up with a workable solution. Sarah agreed to do at least half of her homework every night. If she got a 92 percent or better on her math test, her teacher would give her full credit for the homework assignments. If she got lower than 92 percent, she would agree to complete whichever assignments her teacher deemed necessary.

Sarah kept her end of the bargain. Some nights she did *more* than half of the homework, because now she knew she was only doing what she needed to do in order to master the concept. She never did fall below a 92 percentile on any math test the rest of the year.

The Problem

The child won't stay at a task for more than a few minutes.

What Do You Need to Accomplish?

I need for him to learn to focus on one thing at a time.

An Alternative

Provide him with some options. Decide what needs to be done, then offer one or two ways to do it. Let him switch ways in the middle if he wants to, and let him keep on the move whenever possible while doing the task. Insist he do only one thing at a time, even if he quickly switches from one task to another. Help him identify which method he is using each time he changes direction.

What Do You Need to Accomplish?

I need for him to do it *my* way!

An Alternative

As parents, we have to admit that sometimes it's just plain easier for us if our children will do it our way. Try explaining to your child *why* you think your way will work, then offer to let your child try another method as long as he can prove his way will accomplish the same goal. The hardest part of this suggestion is the patience and tolerance it may take on your part to let your child try out the alternatives!

Combining the Alternatives for Getting a Child to Stay at a Task

I received a letter several years ago from a mother who attended one of my seminars. It remains one of my very favorites because it illustrates how one mom discovered the value of letting her son choose his own way to accomplish a goal. This mother writes:

> Style awareness has changed our lives. I look for ways to
> have Dan be creatively successful. We have a small farm, and

Dan has an acre he has begrudgingly taken care of for four years. He waters with a hose and sprinkler. It's a real pain, and he tells me so regularly. I suggested he brainstorm solutions to the watering problem and then make a list of the five ways he thought he could do better. He would then "sell" his choice to me. We have two greenhouses (25' x 50') we no longer use. He suggested a water system using salvaged plastic pipe from the greenhouses. I thought it was a great idea, provided (a) he could do it with materials we had, and (b) it would wet the whole garden all at once or in sequence. I suggested he play with hoses and sprinklers to see what the pump capacity was. He's 11 years old. He agreed and worked at it for a week.

It took a whole week of devotion, commitment, and an expressed need for privacy. He used about six times the pipe I would have used, and I'm *sure* every T, union, plug, and clamp on the property. But he did it all by himself, and it *does* water the whole acre in three rotations. The middle set spells his name when the water comes on. The system is as unique as Dan!

Don't fall into the trap of believing your child is smart and successful only if he or she does well in the traditional classroom. There are *many* ways of being smart. If you as a parent can help your child discover areas of intelligence and then reinforce that intelligence, you help build your child's confidence and abilities more than you could ever have imagined. Even if you believe your child is suffering from a legitimate learning disability or disorder, you can greatly increase your child's chances of success by determining natural learning style strengths and deciding how much of his frustration and difficulty is a matter of learning style differences and how much is a genuinely physical or emotional problem.

David was an angry, rebellious 15 year old. His parents were at the end of their rope. They had had conferences with teachers, counseled with psychologists, conferred with medical specialists, and prayed with clergy. They had tried punishment, rewards, discussion, threats, and ultimatums. Instead of improving, David steadily become more out of control. When David ran away for the third time in six months and was arrested for shoplifting, his parents were ready to take drastic action. They arranged to have him involuntarily committed to a youth facility where he would be locked up 24 hours a day. There he would undergo a regimented program designed to instill respect and appropriate behaviors through strict authoritarian discipline.

Just before David's scheduled commitment, his parents attended my seminar about learning styles. When they heard about the strong-willed, Concrete Random style, they immediately recognized their son. As they discovered how the CR mind works and identified strategies for motivating and disciplining a CR, their approach with David began to change. During the last seminar session when they were asked how they were doing with David, they made a statement that startled the rest of the group.

"Last night we asked David to forgive us." They went on to explain. "We told him we were sorry for not taking into account his *design*. We don't apologize for the outcomes we've expected, but we realize now that we could have handled many situations in ways that respected how his mind works. We could have helped him know how valued he is as a member of our family."

In the days and weeks that followed, David's parents talked to him about bottom lines, about outcomes and consequences. Then they gave David the opportunity to tell them what *he* could live with and what he couldn't. With the help of an understanding counselor, they are beginning a healing process that will make them a family again.

David realizes that he still must pay the consequences for his rebellion and criminal behavior. Although the youth facility is a very effective program for some styles, David's parents recognized that the program's approach would likely work backwards for David's style. With David's input and the counselor's help, they have found a rehabilitation program that makes sense to his CR nature. Progress is slow and sometimes painful, but David and his parents are convinced that recognizing and appreciating different styles is helping them put their family back together again.

So much of what we parents perceive as our children's deliberate attempts to annoy and frustrate us are actually a difference in approach and perspective. If we can learn to discern what is a learning style difference and how much is true disobedience or defiance, we will be much wiser parents.

I was conducting a seminar at a retreat for day-care teachers and staff. We had divided the group into randoms and sequentials, and I asked both groups the same question.

"If you could never have another raise in pay, what could your organization do to keep you happily working?"

The answer was almost unanimous: "Don't make us work with any 'difficult children.' "

When I asked them to define the "difficult child," the contrast between the groups was very evident. The sequential teachers claimed that the difficult children were those who were so random that they couldn't seem to follow the simplest directions. These children were spontaneous, unpredictable, and often disorganized.

The random teachers disagreed with the others. They claimed that difficult children were the more sequential ones. They were picky and structured, and they never seemed to "lighten up." These sequential children demanded predictable schedules and prompt attention to detail.

In the end, we all came to the same important conclusion. There really isn't a definitive "difficult child." The child who is most difficult is the one who doesn't think like we do!

In a Nutshell

We have spent quite a bit of time in this book trying to identify the consistent patterns of individual learning styles. Although we can learn to accommodate many of those styles, we'll never really be able to neatly label or categorize anyone. Because each human being is so complex, we may never fully appreciate all our differences.

It's never been more important to help our children succeed in a world that is often difficult to understand. It can make a difference with *your* children if you will devote time and energy to discovering *the way they learn.*

Endnotes

Chapter Two

1. Order the *Adult Style Delineator* from Anthony F. Gregorc, 15 Doubleday Rd, Columbia, Connecticut 06237 or call (203) 228-0093.

Chapter Seven

1. Kenneth and Rita Dunn are the authors of several books (see bibliography) and editors for *Learning Styles Network*. Contact: The Center for the Study of Learning Styles, St. John's University, Jamaica, N.Y.

Chapter Eight

1. *The Swassing-Barbe Modality Index*. Administered individually, 20 minutes, all ages, patterns are presented in each modality and must be retained and repeated. Available from Zaner-Bloser, Inc., Columbus, Ohio.

Chapter Nine

1. Herman A. Witkin, "Cognitive Styles in the Educational Setting," *New York University Education Quarterly*, 1977, pp. 14-20.

   Herman A. Witkin et. al., "Field Dependent and Field-Independent Cognitive Styles and Their Educational Implications," *Review of Educational Research*, Winter 1977, vol. 47, No. 1, pp. 1-64.

An Introductory Annotated Bibliography for Parents

Armstrong, Thomas. *In Their Own Way*. New York: St. Martin's Press, 1987.

The first book of a man who, after being a learning disabilities specialist for 16 years, decided there was really no such thing as a "learning disability." He challenges the traditional way of schooling, and gives hope and practical suggestions for parents who believe their children *can* learn, but must do it in their own way.

Armstrong, Thomas. *7 Kinds of Smart*. New York: Penguin Books, 1993.

Armstrong's latest and perhaps most enlightening book. Using Howard Gardner's model of Multiple intelligences, he presents easily understood descriptions of the seven intelligences, as well as a list of 25 ways to help your child develop each one.

Barbe, Walter B. *Growing Up Learning*. Washington, D.C.: Acropolis Books, 1985.

Although this book is currently out of print, you'll find your trip to the library to read it well worth your while! The former editor of *Highlights Magazine* shares a wealth of information about auditory, visual, and kinesthetic modalities. You'll find age-appropriate checklists and dozens of suggestions for helping your child learn in many different ways.

Butler, Kathleen. *It's All in Your Mind: A Student's Guide to Learning Style*. The Learner's Dimension, P. O. Box 6, Columbia, CT 06237, 1988.

Using Gregorc's model of learning styles, Dr. Butler has written a workbook for teenagers who want to identify and learn to use their learning styles to be better students.

Chess, Stella, and Alexander Thomas. *Know Your Child*. New York: Basic Books, 1987.

This is a volume packed with evidence (including longitudinal research studies) to prove that each child has his own unique temperament from the beginning to the end of his life. Their "goodness of fit" theory has some very practical applications to successful parenting.

Dobson, James C. *Parenting Isn't for Cowards*. Waco, Tex.: Word Books, 1987.

As always, Dr. Dobson presents a compelling case for parents to understand and appreciate their children. Full of practical advice and encouragement, this book also supports the idea that parents must know and appreciate their child's individual personality and temperament.

Dunn, Rita, Kenneth Dunn and Gary Price. *Learning Style Inventory* (LSI) for students in grades 3-12, and *Productivity Environmental Preference Survey* (PEPS) for adults.

Direct, self-report instruments based on rank ordering of choices for each of 104 items. Computerized scoring is available from Price Systems, Box 3271, Lawrence, Kansas 66044.

Dunn, Rita and Kenneth Dunn. *Teaching Students through Their Individual Learning Styles*. Reston, Vir.: Prentice-Hall, 1978.

A landmark work launching the idea of learning styles through environmental preferences and multisensory modality approaches. This book is an important resource for parents and teachers alike.

Dunn, Rita. Editor *Learning Styles Network*, The Center for Learning and Teaching Styles, St. John's University, Jamaica, New York.

The Learning Styles Network publishes a newsletter, an extensive annotated bibliography, and various materials on learning styles—especially suitable for educators.

Gregorc, Anthony D. *An Adult's Guide to Style*. Columbia, Conn.: Gregorc Associates, 1982.

The definitive volume for identifying and understanding Gregorc's model of learning styles. Packed with definitions and examples, you'll find this book an invaluable reference for serious study.

Keirsey, David and Marilyn Bates. *Please Understand Me: Character and Temperment Types*. Del Mar, Calif.: Prometheus, Nemesis, 1978.

This book provides a fascinating look at personality type and temperament. You'll discover how your temperament affects your success in relationships, careers, and life in general.

Kroeger, Otto and Janet M. Thuesen. *Type Talk*. New York: Delacorte Press, 1988.

This is a fun, easy-to-read guide to the Myers-Briggs version of Carl Jung's personality types. Loaded with anecdotes, this book is one you'll find yourself loaning to your friends!

Rusch, Shari Lyn. *Stumbling Blocks to Stepping Stones*. Seattle: Arc Press, 1991.

A touching true story of a little girl growing up with multiple "learning disabilities" who struggled to become successful in spite of a school system that gave little or no help. Full of hope as well as specific suggestions for other children who may be suffering, this book is a valuable resource for parents and teachers.

Swindoll, Charles R. *You and Your Child: A Biblical Guide for Nurturing Confident Children From Infancy to Independence*. Nashville: Thomas Nelson Publishers, 1990.

A compelling and eye-opening book for parents who want to instill lasting moral and spiritual values in their children. Using a scriptural perspective, Dr. Swindoll presents a powerful argument in favor of each child's individuality and value.

Tobias, Cynthia Ulrich and Pat Guild. *No Sweat, How to Use Your Learning Style to Be a Better Student*. Seattle: The Teaching Advisory, 1991.
A handbook for students using the Witkin model for study skills.

Tobias, Cynthia Ulrich. *I Like Your Style!*
A quarterly newsletter filled with practical strategies and up-to-date resources. Published by Learning Styles Unlimited, Inc. Call (206) 874-9141 to subscribe.

Tobias, Cynthia Ulrich with Nick Walker. *"Who's Gonna Make Me?" Effective Strategies for Dealing With the Strong-Willed Child* (video). Seattle: Chuck Snyder & Associates, 1992.
Focusing on the Concrete Random, strong-willed child, this 45-minute video presents practical, hands-on strategies for bringing out the *best* in your strong-willed child. This is one you'll definitely loan to your friends!

Favorite Children's Books

Hazen, Barbara Shook. *Even If I Did Something Awful*. New York: Aladdin, 1992.
A wonderful story of unconditional love without compromising parental authority. Good for all ages!

Henkes, Kevin. *Chester's Way*. New York: Puffin Books, 1988.
A delightful story that shows children how their learning style differences can help them appreciate others for their strengths.

One of my favorite posters reads:

We have not succeeded in solving all of your problems. The answers we have found only serve to raise a whole new set of questions. In some ways, we feel we are as confused as ever, but we believe we are confused on a higher level and about more important things.

—Author unknown

For more information and to obtain Cynthia Tobias as a speaker contact:

Learning Styles Unlimited, Inc.
1911 SW Campus Drive
Suite 370
Federal Way, Washington 98023

Telephone: (206) 874-9141
FAX: (206) 925-5674